How to Ace the National Geographic Bee

Official Study Guide

Fifth Edition

by

Stephen F. Cunha

Washington, D.C.

In memory of John Joseph Ferguson and Ann Judge,
who perished aboard American Airlines Flight 77, which crashed into the Pentagon on September 11, 2001. They were traveling to California with six Washington, D.C., teachers and students as part of an educational field trip sponsored by the National Geographic Society. Joe and Ann were tireless, visionary supporters of the Society's education outreach programs. Their enduring work directly benefits countless teachers and students throughout North America. —SFC

Cover design by Sanjida Rashid

Back cover: National Geographic Bee host Mo Rocca
and National Geographic Society CEO Gary Knell
with Geo Bee contestants in the National Geographic courtyard.

The text type is set in New Caledonia;
headlines are set in Clarendon.

All questions and place-names were accurate and current at the date of their actual use in the National Geographic Bee.

Trade paperback ISBN: 978-1-4263-3080-3
Reinforced library binding ISBN: 978-1-4263-3081-0

Printed in the United States of America
17/WOR/1

Contents

Foreword

I wish I were in fourth grade again. Then I could compete in the National Geographic Bee.

You see, when I was growing up in Bethesda, Maryland, my favorite thing to do after school each day was to pull the encyclopedia volumes (ask your parents what those are) off the shelf, spread them on the family room floor, lie on my stomach on the red carpet, and page through each book, memorizing facts about different countries.

I learned their currencies. (Greece's drachma sounded so dramatic.) I studied their chief exports. (How else would I have known that Turkey is the world's largest source of sour cherries?) I marveled at their shapes. (Chile was so skinny I wondered if people there had to stand sideways to keep from stepping into Argentina.)

But I was especially proud that *I knew the capital of every country in the world.* "Name a country and I'll tell you the capital!" I'd beg my family, friends, and weary restaurant waitstaff. If they asked about Bolivia (two capitals), I'd get a special thrill. If they asked about South Africa (three capitals), my head would practically explode with excitement.

It was quite an accomplishment, if I do say so myself, and one that never really ended. In the early 1990s, when the Soviet Union fell apart, I nearly had a nervous breakdown. All those "Stans"! (My favorite remains Kyrgyzstan's capital, Bishkek. It sounds delicious.)

My world capital prowess didn't just help me stand out as a child. After graduating from college, I took a job at New York City's Macy's department store selling fragrances on commission; the more I'd sell, the more I was paid. Many of the customers were diplomats from the United Nations. I would politely say, "May I ask where you're from?"

"I am from the African nation of Burundi," replied one such diplomat reservedly.

"Oh, are you from ... Bujumbura?" I inquired.

"Why, yes I am!" he said. "How do you know so much about my country?"

And invariably I'd make the sale ... over and over and over again. Yes, world capitals helped me pay my rent.

In 2016, I was honored to host the National Geographic Bee in Washington, D.C. (If you're reading this book, I'm pretty sure you know it's the capital of the United States.) Meeting 54 competitors, all of whom know every world capital, felt like home.

More importantly, I discovered how deep the study of geography goes. (Deeper even than Siberia's Lake Baikal, which is the deepest lake in ... well, you know.) It's about so much more than memorization. The 10 extraordinarily impressive finalists were able to call upon their knowledge of the planet's cartography, climate, culture, and more—and answer not just the "where" and "what" questions but also the "why" questions.

And I happen to know *why* you're reading this study guide. It's because you're curious about the world. You care about the world. And for that, all of the rest of us thank you.

Now if you'll excuse me, I've got some studying to do. I'm hosting again this year and really don't want to get shown up by a fourth grader.

Mo Rocca
Host, National Geographic Bee

1

The Why of Where: Defining Geography

As globalization is increasing, understanding about the world is a very important thing for everyone, and National Geographic is providing an opportunity for kids to learn more about our great planet.
—SAKETH JONNALAGADDA, 2016 NATIONAL RUNNER-UP

Imagine captaining a 17th-century merchant ship with a crew of 200 and a cargo hold stuffed with exotic goods from the Far East. You are London-bound to exchange your booty for gold coins and more shipping contracts from anxious merchants. Gazing across the Indian Ocean at sunrise, you take stock of the possible hazards that threaten success: pirates, sudden storms, rocky coastlines, and even mutiny. But the biggest danger of all is veering off course into an endless sea because you cannot plot your location accurately on the map.

Before John Harrison developed a special clock called the marine chronometer in the mid-1700s, sailors could not pinpoint their longitude—their location east or west of the prime meridian. Captains routinely lost hundreds of men and tons of cargo to starvation and storms while searching for a place to land. In Dava Sobel's wonderful book Longitude, *the author describes a dozen disasters,* including that of Admiral Sir Clowdisley Shovell. The admiral lost four of his five warships and 2,000 troops in 1707 after misjudging his longitude in the Scilly Isles, off the southwestern tip of England. Adrift in dense fog, the ships "pricked themselves on rocks and went down like stones." Yikes!

Fortunately, Harrison's ingenious clock enabled navigators to determine longitude by comparing the time of day on board ship with noon in Greenwich, England, which was (and still is) located on the prime meridian (0° longitude). Because latitude—the distance north or south of the Equator—was easy to calculate by observing the stars, sailors could now see where their latitude and longitude intersected on the map and determine their exact geographic location in an open ocean where there are no landmarks. (You'll learn more about latitude and longitude in Chapter 3.)

Early continental explorers also suffered when they lacked geographical information. Poor Hannibal crossed the Alps in the wrong time of year and nearly froze to death. Lewis and Clark almost perished in the mountains of Idaho and Montana because they didn't know how vast the Rocky Mountains were. And what were those Vikings thinking when they attempted to grow barley in Iceland a thousand years ago?

Knowing where places are located is an important first step to learning geography and enjoying the Bee. Fortunately for us, using maps and finding latitude and longitude are much easier today than during poor Sir Clowdisley Shovell's lifetime.

However, geography is much more than places on a map. In the words of Alexander Graham Bell, one of the founders of the

National Geographic Society, geography is "the world and all that is in it." Place-names such as Brazil, Stockholm, Mount Everest, and Yangtze River are to geography what the alphabet is to reading. They open the gate for boundless and lifelong learning. Knowing where places are on a map is important, but the real heart of geography is understanding why people settle in a particular place, who their neighbors are, how they make a living, why they dress and speak the way they do, and what they do for fun. Developing this sense of place will raise a flat map to life.

Geographers investigate our global climate, landforms, economies, political systems, human cultures, and migration patterns. They are concerned not just with where something is located, but also with why it is there and how it relates to other things. A good geographer knows how to combine this information from many different sources and how to identify patterns that can help us understand our complex world. Geography explains why your grandmother moved to Tucson (warm and dry climate), how oil from Kuwait reaches Italy (by way of the Suez Canal), where tropical rain forests grow (near the Equator), who faces toward Mecca as they pray (Muslims), and which continent is the most populated (Asia). In a nutshell, geography is the "Why of Where" science that blends and enriches history, literature, mathematics, and science.

Although place-names of the world are now thoroughly mapped and available in atlases, maps, books, and even online, knowing where you are and the geographic characteristics of that place is just as important today as in earlier times.

Understanding people and environments influences the location of everything from Walmarts to hospitals to software manufacturing plants. City planners need population projections and environmental data before they can approve plans to build housing developments, office buildings, and shopping centers. Engineers must study water resources and the lay of the land before starting any project. (Even a small hill or creek can greatly increase construction costs.) Imagine trying to advertise a new product without knowing the composition (Hispanic, African American, Asian, European), age structure (teenagers or grandparents), and economic characteristics (farmers, factory workers, or professionals) of the people you want to buy it. Highway construction cannot proceed until facts about climate, soil, vegetation, and the number of people who will drive the proposed route are considered. Each day, kids everywhere awake in sheets of woven Egyptian cotton, pull on clothes stitched in Bangladesh, wolf down bananas grown in Central America, and grab schoolbooks printed in Singapore to board buses assembled in Michigan from parts made in Japan and Germany.

For more than a decade, the growth of our global society—the rising dependence of nations upon one another for trade and security—has made geographical studies more important than ever. Acronyms and abbreviations—such as NAFTA, GATT, EU, and WTO—are heard on the evening news. Schools from Alaska to Zambia stress second-language and culture studies to better prepare their students not just for a global economy but also for a more crowded planet where migration, tourism, and the

Internet connect our global family more each day. The global war on terrorism further underscores the great importance of more fully understanding the people of the world, how they live, what they believe, and the environment and resources we share.

Whether you are the secretary of state for the United States or the secretary of your class, knowing geography will help you understand the world.

2

Bee Basics: Understanding the Contest

Through the Bee, I have become much more aware of the world around me, the problems that are facing it, and what can be done to solve these issues.
—SHRIYA YARLAGADDA, 2015 NATIONAL RUNNER-UP

This chapter marches through the annual Bee calendar from registration to the national finals. It explains who is eligible to participate and the format at the school, state, and national levels. (It is important to note that although the Bee provides an instruction booklet to each registered school, the booklet contains recommended procedures only. Schools sometimes have to make adjustments to fit their needs.) Understanding how the Bee works and following the advice at the end of the chapter will help you relax, have fun, and perform better.

REGISTRATION

Registering is easy. Schools must register each year by the deadline (usually mid-January). Registration fees are $100 until mid-December and $120 until registration closes. Check with school officials to see if your school is entered for the upcoming Bee or look for your school on our website under the registration link. If you are a middle school student who rotates among classes, the social studies teacher is the best person to ask, followed by the principal. Schools must register *each* year by the deadline. More information on Bee registration appears on page 123 and on our website: natgeobee.org.

ELIGIBILITY

All U.S. schools with any of the grades four through eight may register for the Bee. Students enrolled in a conventional public or private school may not compete as part of a homeschool Bee. Homeschooling associations may register to have a county or area-wide Bee for homeschoolers in their area. A student may compete in a magnet school Bee only if enrolled full-time at the magnet school. Parents and teachers must pay close attention to these details to prevent a disqualification.

Students who are not over the age of 15 by September 1 of that school year may participate. The Bee is an open contest that does not separate students into age or grade-level categories. There must be a minimum of six student participants in a school to hold a school-level competition. Students may participate in no more than five years of the Bee.

SCHOOL-LEVEL BEES

In mid-October, Bee packets are available for download to registered schools. The packet contains the suggested procedures and the question booklet. A certificate and a medal for the school champion are mailed to registered schools. School officials then select the days for their Bee, so long as the competition falls within the dates established by the Society—normally anytime between early October and early February.

School Bees are the responsibility of the schools. Their decisions are final. These Bees are usually broken into a Preliminary Competition, which normally takes place in individual classrooms, and the Final Competition, which is often held in the school assembly room (cafeteria, auditorium, gym, etc.).

Preliminary Competition

These rounds usually require an oral response. A teacher or other moderator reads the questions aloud. You will be asked one question per round and will have 15 seconds to answer each question. To keep the contest moving, you are allowed to ask to have a question repeated or a word spelled only two times during the Preliminary Competition. Such a request to the moderator must be made immediately.

Once the question has been repeated or the word spelled, you will have the remainder of your 15 seconds to answer the question. You must start to give your answer before the 15-second time limit is up. If you do not answer within the allotted time, the moderator will say, "Time," give the correct answer, and move on to the next student. One point is awarded for each correct response; a pass is counted as an incorrect response. There is no penalty for mispronunciations (or misspellings, in the event of a written response) so long as the moderator can determine you know the correct answer. The student with the most correct answers wins the chance to advance to the Final Round.

Tiebreakers

If there are ties in determining the finalists, officials will use a series of Preliminary Competition Tiebreaker Questions. Everyone involved begins with a clean slate—no hits and no misses. Students get the same question and write their answers on the paper provided. Again, there is no penalty for misspellings so long as the moderator can determine that the correct answer has been given. Questioning continues until the tie or ties have been broken.

Final Competition

The Final Competition consists of a Final Round and a Championship Round. If you are lucky enough to advance to this level, you may find yourself on a stage in the school auditorium. As with any contest or game, the pressure builds as you progress up the ladder. Expect some bright lights and audience noise, ranging from restrained gasps to thunderous applause.

In addition to the round-robin oral questions in the Preliminary Competition, the Final Round includes questions that require written responses (students are simultaneously asked the same question and respond by writing their answers on the paper provided). Other questions may involve graphs, maps, or photographs. If so, you will be given a copy of the visual to study up close before answering the question. But the biggest difference between the Preliminary Competition and the Final Round is that students are eliminated after giving their second incorrect answer. Once the third-place winner has been determined, the remaining two students advance to the Championship Round.

Championship Round

In the Championship Round, the two contestants start with a clean slate. Both are asked the same questions simultaneously and given 15 seconds to write their answers. The moderator then asks the students for their answers. The student with the most correct answers wins the school Bee. Tiebreaker questions may be necessary to determine the winner. The champion receives a medal and a certificate from the National Geographic Society, and every student who entered the school Bee receives a Certificate of Participation.

QUALIFYING TEST

To advance to the state Bee as a representative of his or her school, the school winner must take the online Qualifying Test. To access this test, the teacher administering the test must log into his or her registration account at natgeobee.org for the student to take the test online. This test should be given in a quiet location in the school building. It must be monitored by a teacher who is not a parent or guardian of the school Bee winner. The test has about 70 multiple-choice questions, covering the entire range of geographic inquiry, including a set that pertains to a map, table, or graph. There is a time limit of one hour. The test must be completed by the deadline, which is usually no later than the first week of February.

The National Geographic Society scores one Qualifying Test from each participating school. The top 100 students (more if there are ties) from each of the 50 states, the District of Columbia, the Department of Defense Dependents Schools, and the Atlantic and Pacific territories compete in their respective state

Bees. The National Geographic Society appoints state Bee coordinators to coordinate this portion of the contest. In early March, Society officials notify the teachers of the students who qualify for the state competition.

The state Bees can be held late March or early April. An adult must accompany each student to the state Bee. In most cases this is a teacher, parent, or legal guardian. Other adults may substitute with school approval. Expect the Bee to begin with an opening assembly jam-packed with all 100 state finalists, officials, teachers, and a zillion family members. The room is abuzz with excitement and nervous anticipation.

The contestants break into five groups of 20 students. The seating and room assignments are determined by random drawing before the Bee. Just as in the school-level competition, there are preliminary, final, and championship rounds (and tiebreakers if necessary). The Final and Championship Rounds are held in front of a large audience and are very exciting. Some rounds will include questions that require written responses on a sheet of paper. You should also expect questions that require interpreting information from a visual. This may be a photograph, illustration, map, satellite photo (e.g., from Google Earth), data table, or graph that is displayed on a large screen. You will be given a copy of the visual to study up close before answering the question. Once the Bee is under way, you will impress yourself with how many questions you can answer correctly! The same procedure that is recommended to schools for determining the school-level winners is used to determine the state champions. The winner of each state Bee wins a trip to Washington, D.C., to compete in the national-level Bee.

THE NATIONAL-LEVEL BEE

State Bee winners meet at the headquarters of the National Geographic Society, in Washington, D.C., in May to compete for the title of national champion. The format for the national-level preliminary competition is similar to that of previous levels with rounds of questions, but there is an additional component called a GeoChallenge that is scored by a panel of judges. In general, the questions are harder, and there are more rounds involving visuals, such as photographs, maps, and graphs. The top ten winners of the Preliminary Competition compete in the Final Round. The format of the Final Round is different from earlier levels of the Bee. Instead of being eliminated after two incorrect answers, students earn points for correct answers and are eliminated at various checkpoints based on the lowest scores. The Final Round also includes GeoChallenge questions that are scored by a panel of judges. The Championship Round is similar to previous levels, with the top two students starting with a clean slate. Journalist and humorist Mo Rocca is the moderator for the Final and Championship Rounds. It's always fun to follow along and see how many questions you can answer; check the Bee website for broadcast information. The top three finishers take home college scholarships, and the champion also earns a prize trip. The total prize and scholarship monies awarded at the school, state, and national levels make the Bee one of the richest academic competitions on Earth.

The Canadian equivalent of the National Geographic Bee also features a series of competitions at the school, provincial or territorial, and national levels that are designed to test students' knowledge and skills in geography.

Currently there are two grade levels to the Challenge: Level 1 for grades four to six and Level 2 for grades seven to ten. Teachers register online for the Challenge; any number of students or classes within a school may compete. All registered schools receive an online instruction booklet, question and answer booklet, and prizes. The information is available in English and French.

The competition for Level 1 students ends at the school level. When the top student has been determined at the school level in Level 2 (this must be determined by the end of February), he or she will take the provincial/territorial online test to see if they will be invited to the national final. The top student in each province and territory will be recognized with a prize. The highest scoring students from this competition compete in the National Final in May. The top three scorers are declared the Canadian National Champions and receive scholarships.

BEE GREAT: ADVICE TO CONTESTANTS

The following list is the result of more than a decade of "Bee-ing" with students, teachers, and parents. Although my experience has been mostly at the state level, these tips will help at any level in almost any type of competition. They are included here to help make the Bee a truly memorable and fun event.

Relax! Cramming hurts your brain

The evening before and the morning of the Bee are prime times to relax, play with your dog, and go for a bike ride with a sibling or friend. Don't stay up the night before conversing with owls while attempting to cram in a few last-minute facts. This contest is fun, so rest up and dream of faraway lands.

Before then, set aside part of each day to prepare for the Bee. Remember that geography is an integrative subject that takes time to learn and appreciate. Avoid flipping flash cards on the way to the Bee. (Several times I have seen parents quizzing students just moments before the Bee!) This adds tension that can detract from the quality of your performance and your enjoyment of the competition.

Healthy body, healthy mind

Whether you live in Paris, Pyongyang, or Philadelphia, the best advice is to stay fit, eat a balanced diet, and avoid spending so much time hunting for facts online or looking things up in books that your physical fitness declines. A healthy body houses a sharper and more capable mind.

Many students at every level of the Bee find that eating before the contest is a difficult idea to stomach. Yet your brain is a big muscle, and to keep it working at full throttle requires high-octane fuel. That is to say, CHOW DOWN BEFORE THE BEE! Don't arrive hungry. An empty stomach will make any jitters you have feel much worse. This problem does not affect every student, but if you know that big events—even the fun ones—make it difficult to eat, then here is some food for thought.

First, eat a well-balanced dinner the night before the Bee. This way, unless your stomach is the size of a thimble, you'll have calories in your tank at least through noon the following day. Second, eat at least a small breakfast that includes some juice and something solid, such as fruit, carbohydrates (toast, muffins, cereal), or eggs. Try to avoid greasy and high-fat foods, as they are harder to digest and can make your tummy do backflips.

Dress for success

Although this is a special event, you don't need to rent a tux or a frilly evening gown. Even ties and dresses are rare. Most kids pull on something comfortable. Pants or a skirt with a clean shirt or blouse are a good choice. Of course, you'll want to look neat—advancing to the finals at any level could land you onstage.

Take a deep breath

It's easy to panic when you hear a question that freaks you out! "Oh no, I can't remember the largest city on Mars!" Forgetting to breathe or taking several gasps is a natural reaction. If this occurs, relax, take a deep breath, collect your thoughts, and then look for clues in the question that will help you figure out the correct answer. Remember, you have 15 seconds (except in the national finals) to answer. Believe it or not, that's a long time! Failing to take in oxygen will make it more difficult to think and will increase that feeling of alarm!

Listen to every question in each round

When competing in the oral rounds, listen to every question and every answer. You may pick up clues that will help you come up with the right answer when it's your turn.

Stand by your first answer

Unless you are certain of an error, stick with the first answer that comes to mind. Believe it or not, studies show that students who change their answers or get stuck trying to choose between two answers usually select a less accurate choice the second time.

Ignore your friends

While you're competing, don't look at people you know, especially just before and during your turn. Ask your friends, teacher, parents, and other family members to make themselves invisible by sitting as far away as possible. Also, tell them to photograph you *after* the Bee, not while you are trying to remember which country borders Zimbabwe on the east. (Mozambique, of course!)

Speak loudly and write with a big stick

Make your answers known in very decisive ways. Speak in a loud, clear voice. When a written answer is required, write clearly in LARGE, BOLD LETTERS. The teacher/moderator must be able to understand your answer and read your handwriting.

Remember: It is impossible to fail in the Bee. Just by taking part you are already a success!

CHAPTER 3

Top Ten Study Tips

Since all aspects of geography are interconnected, finding something you love to study will make it easier and more interesting to learn new things.
—NEELAM SANDHU, NATIONAL GEOGRAPHIC WORLD GEOGRAPHY CHAMPION (TEAM), 2013

The ten trusty tips outlined in this chapter will help you "Bee" ready. This powerful advice has been assembled over many years from students just like you. A small army of teachers added their two cents' worth, too.

Don't expect to learn everything about geography in just one school year. Remember that you are eligible to enter the Bee from the fourth through the eighth grade. No one expects a fourth grader to know as much as an eighth grader, but it's not impossible. Susannah Batko-Yovino was only a sixth grader when she became the national champion in 1990! By participating each year, you will increase your knowledge of geography and self-confidence. These ten study tips will teach you the basics and how to build on them to recognize geographic patterns. You'll be thinking like a geographer in no time!

Choose Your Tools

Getting started in geography is easy if you have the right tools. Spending a part of each day with these tools will expand your world in a hurry. A few pointers on using these are presented here. Advice about specific products and where to find them appears in Chapter 6.

A large **WORLD MAP** should be in every home. Concentrate first on learning the continents, oceans, and largest islands. Then focus on countries, capital cities, and major physical features (such as mountain ranges, lakes, and rivers), gradually adding other places and features to your vocabulary. Hang your world map next to your bed or on the closet door. Put smaller maps of each continent around your house. Position one in the bathroom so you can learn the countries of Africa while brushing your teeth. Laminated map place mats let you explore Italy while slurping spaghetti. You can also tape maps behind the front seat of your family car and visit South America on the way to school.

A good **ATLAS** is the next essential tool. These come in all sizes, with many excellent and reasonably priced volumes to match your skill level. Be sure to use one that is less than five years old so that it includes important name updates.

Look for three other features when choosing an atlas. First, it should have both physical maps (emphasizing natural features) and political maps (emphasizing country boundaries and cities). Second, make sure it includes an index (or gazetteer) that alphabetically lists place-names that appear on the maps. This will help you find unfamiliar locations. Finally, look for text that includes information about each continent, country, and world region (such as Southeast Asia or Middle America), plus a section on geographic comparisons (longest rivers, largest cities, etc.).

BLANK OUTLINE MAPS are the third tool. These black-and-white line maps outline the continents and countries. Important physical features such as major rivers and mountain ranges may also appear. See Chapter 6 for tips on finding these maps online. Practice labeling countries, cities, rivers, mountains, and other geographic information as you learn it. Always start with the most obvious features and then add more detailed information as you progress. Blank maps are a great way to quiz yourself.

A **GEOGRAPHY REFERENCE BOOK** is another important tool. Although maps and atlases help you learn where Mongolia, Mauna Loa, and other places are located, a good geography reference book explains *why* they are located there, *who* lives there, *what* they do, and *how* the landscape came to be. These books usually arrange information in alphabetical order either by single topic (Agriculture, Alluvial Fan, Avalanche), or by category (Earth Science, Population, Wildlife). The most helpful ones enrich the text with numerous maps, photographs, charts and graphs, and a glossary of terms. A good reference book takes you to the next level of geographic learning by bringing maps to life. This marks the point where memorization evolves into real geographic exploration and discovery!

SATELLITE IMAGE SOURCES such as NASA's Visible Earth and the U.S. Geological Survey's EarthExplorer will round out your tool kit. Learning to maneuver about and interpret satellite images will help you visualize and build the mental maps described in Tip #4.

A good map is worth a thousand pictures. Expert map readers can absorb oceans of geographic information in a short time. But to understand all that a map can tell you, you must first learn the language of maps.

LATITUDE and **LONGITUDE** are the imaginary lines that divide Earth's surface into a grid. Under this system, both latitude and longitude are measured in terms of the 360 degrees of a circle. The latitude and longitude of a place are its **COORDINATES.** Coordinates mark the **ABSOLUTE LOCATION** of a place. Understanding coordinates, you can use a map to locate any point on Earth.

Latitude is the distance north or south of the **EQUATOR,** the line of 0° latitude that divides Earth into two equal halves called hemispheres. The top half is the **NORTHERN HEMISPHERE,** and the bottom half is the **SOUTHERN HEMISPHERE.** Lines of latitude are also called **PARALLELS** because they circle Earth without ever touching each other. From the Equator we measure latitude north and south to the poles. The **NORTH POLE** is located at 90° north latitude, and the **SOUTH POLE** is located at 90° south latitude.

There are other important parallels that you should learn. The parallel of latitude 23° 30' north of the Equator is called the **TROPIC OF CANCER,** and the parallel 23° 30' south of the Equator is the **TROPIC OF CAPRICORN.** The region between these two parallels is called the **TROPICS.** The **SUBTROPICS** are the zones located between 23° 30' and about 40° north and south of the Equator.

The parallel of latitude 66° 30' north of the Equator is called the **ARCTIC CIRCLE,** and the parallel 66° 30' south of the Equator is the **ANTARCTIC CIRCLE.** The region between 66° 30' N and 90° N is called the Arctic; the region between 66° 30' S and 90° S is called the Antarctic. Both regions can simply be called polar.

Longitude is the distance east or west of the **PRIME MERIDIAN,** the point of 0° longitude. This is also the starting place for measuring distance both east and west around the globe. Lines of longitude are called **MERIDIANS.** They also circle Earth, but they converge at the poles.

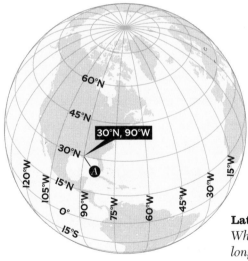

Latitude and Longitude
When used together, latitude and longitude form a grid that provides a system for determining the exact, or absolute, location of every place on Earth. For example, the absolute location of point A is 30° N, 90° W.

We also use the coordinate system to determine direction. When you face the North Pole (90° N), the sun rises to your right (east) and sets to your left (west). The south is behind you. These four points—north, south, east, and west—are **CARDINAL DIRECTIONS.** Any point *between* two cardinal directions is an **INTERMEDIATE DIRECTION.** For example, looking north and partly to the east is said to be looking northeast. But if you turn around and glance south and partly to the west, you are looking southwest.

A **GLOBE** is the only accurate representation of our spherical Earth. Think of a globe as a scale model of Earth with a paper or plastic map mounted on its spherical surface. Globes are great to study because, unlike most flat maps, they show continents and oceans in their true proportions. Size, shape, distance, and direction are all accurately represented. Projecting this round shape onto a flat sheet of paper to make a map distorts these elements. To solve the problem of distortion, mapmakers use a variety of **MAP PROJECTIONS** to portray our curved Earth on a flat sheet of paper. Each projection distorts Earth according to a mathematical calculation. Three commonly used projections are the Mercator, the Winkel Tripel, and the Goode's Interrupted Homolosine. The **MERCATOR** projection is helpful to navigators because it allows them to maintain a constant compass direction as they travel between two points, but it greatly exaggerates areas at higher latitudes. The **WINKEL TRIPEL** is a general-purpose projection popularly used for political, physical, and thematic maps because it minimizes distortion of both size and shape. The

GOODE'S INTERRUPTED HOMOLOSINE minimizes distortion of scale and shape by interrupting the globe. This type of equal-area projection is useful for mapping comparisons of various kinds of data, such as rain forests and population density.

MERCATOR

WINKEL TRIPEL

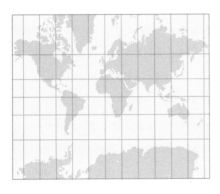

GOODE'S INTERRUPTED HOMOLOSINE

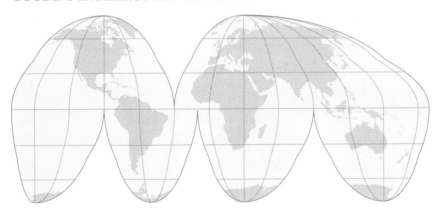

There are two main types of maps. **PHYSICAL MAPS** emphasize natural features such as mountains, rivers, lakes, deserts, and plains. Mapmakers often use shades of color to indicate different elevations. **POLITICAL MAPS** use lines to show boundaries between countries, points to show cities, and various other symbols to show roads, airports, canals, and other human-related features. Examples of these two kinds of maps are on the opposite page.

We use latitude and longitude to determine the absolute location of physical and political features and **RELATIVE LOCATION** to explain the underlying reasons for that precise location and to show the interconnection of geographic phenomena.

For example, the geographic grid pinpoints Chicago's absolute location at 41° N, 87° W. However, the Windy City's location on the shore of Lake Michigan is *relative* to the historic water commerce routes favored by early Native Americans and settlers. Without Lake Michigan, Chicago might not exist.

Similarly, Khartoum, the capital city of Sudan, is located at 15° N, 32° E, *relative* to the confluence of the Blue and the White Niles. Without the confluence of rivers, this city would not have become such an important economic center.

Physical features are located relative to the geologic processes that created them. For example, Mount Rainier, in Washington State, is located at 47° N, 122° W, relative to the two tectonic plates (moving slabs of Earth's crust) that created the Cascade Range. As a result, Mount Rainier shares the same geologic origin as the other volcanoes located north and south of it. Without the tectonic plate boundary, this part of the Pacific Northwest might

PHYSICAL MAP

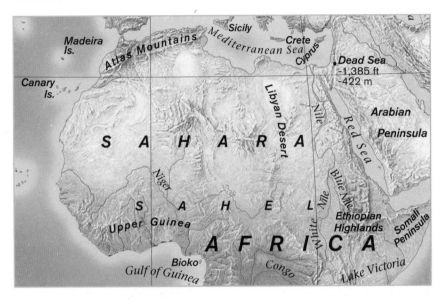

POLITICAL MAP

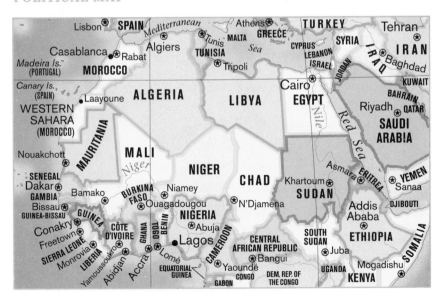

IMAGINARY LANDSCAPE

1 Volcano

2 Strait

3 Sound

4 Peninsula

5 Isthmus

6 Spit

7 Lagoon

8 Bay

9 Delta

10 Divide

11 Reservoir

12 Glacier

13 Desert

14 Mesa

15 Canyon

have a much different physical environment and human settle-ment pattern than we see today.

Use the world maps, atlases, and geographic reference books in your tool kit to learn more about these concepts and the language of maps. They are the building blocks for more learning and the source of many Bee questions.

The diagram of an imaginary landscape on the opposite page was used in a round of questions in a state-level Bee to quiz students on their ability to identify physical features. Students were asked to give the number that best represented a specific physical feature. Of course, they didn't have the benefit of being able to see the answers! They are provided for you so that you can use this as a study tool for learning some very basic physical terms. You will find definitions for each of these terms in your geographic reference book. Learn them and try to find examples of each on physical maps. You can be sure that geographic terms are a frequent topic for Bee questions.

TIP

3

Study the A "Bee" Cs

Once you know how to read maps, the next step is to learn the most important place-names that go on them. This memorization develops your global sense of place. Learning place-names is like learning your ABCs. Without knowing the alphabet, you can't spell words. Without knowing place-names, you can't identify places and features on a map or understand the interrelationships between physical and human activities. Place-names are a necessary and important building block to greater geographic knowledge.

The number of place-names can be overwhelming. Organizing them into physical and political groups can be helpful. Start with the first categories in each group and work your way down. Don't just memorize a list of names and figures. Find each feature or place on the map and take time to learn about it and what it's near.

PHYSICAL FEATURES

THE CONTINENTS

| | AREA | | % of |
	(sq mi)	(sq km)	Earth's land
Asia	17,208,000	44,570,000	30.0
Africa	11,608,000	30,065,000	20.2
North America	9,449,000	24,474,000	16.5
South America	6,880,000	17,819,000	12.0
Antarctica	5,100,000	13,209,000	8.9
Europe	3,841,000	9,947,000	6.7
Australia	2,970,000	7,692,000	5.2

THE OCEANS

| | AREA | | % of Earth's |
	(sq mi)	(sq km)	water area
Pacific	65,436,200	169,479,000	46.8
Atlantic	35,338,500	91,526,400	25.3
Indian	29,839,800	74,694,800	20.6
Arctic	5,390,000	13,960,100	3.9

Note: The tables at the bottom of the previous page list the names of the continents and oceans in order by size. Although some geographers consider Europe and Asia as one continent called Eurasia, National Geographic counts them as two landmasses to make a total of seven continents. Likewise, some maps show a Southern Ocean around Antarctica. Others show this body of water as the continuation of the Atlantic, Pacific, and Indian Oceans.

HIGHEST POINT ON EACH CONTINENT

	feet	meters
Everest, Asia	29,035	8,850
Aconcagua, S. America	22,831	6,959
Denali (McKinley), N. America	20,310	6,190
Kilimanjaro, Africa	19,340	5,895
El'brus, Europe	18,510	5,642
Vinson Massif, Antarctica	16,066	4,897
Kosciuszko, Australia	7,310	2,228

LOWEST POINT ON EACH CONTINENT

	feet	meters
Bentley Subglacial Trench, Antarctica	-8,383	-2,555
Dead Sea, Asia	-1,385	-422
Lake Assal, Africa	-512	-156
Laguna del Carbón, S. America	-344	-105
Death Valley, N. America	-282	-86
Caspian Sea, Europe	-92	-28
Lake Eyre, Australia	-52	-16

TEN LARGEST SEAS

	AREA (sq mi)	(sq km)
Coral	1,615,260	4,183,510
South China	1,388,570	3,596,390
Caribbean	1,094,330	2,834,290
Bering	972,810	2,519,580
Mediterranean	953,320	2,469,100
Sea of Okhotsk	627,490	1,625,190
Gulf of Mexico	591,430	1,531,810
Norwegian	550,300	1,425,280
Greenland	447,050	1,157,850
Sea of Japan (East Sea)	389,290	1,008,260

TEN LARGEST LAKES

	AREA (sq mi)	(sq km)
Caspian Sea, Europe-Asia	143,200	371,000
Superior, N. America	31,700	82,100
Victoria, Africa	26,800	69,500
Huron, N. America	23,000	59,600
Michigan, N. America	22,300	57,800
Tanganyika, Africa	12,600	32,600
Baikal, Asia	12,200	31,500
Great Bear, N. America	12,100	31,300
Malawi, Africa	11,200	28,900
Great Slave, N. America	11,000	28,600

TEN LARGEST ISLANDS

	AREA				AREA	
	(sq mi)	(sq km)			(sq mi)	(sq km)
Greenland	836,000	2,166,000	Sumatra		165,000	427,300
New Guinea	306,000	792,500	Honshu		87,800	227,400
Borneo	280,100	725,500	Great Britain		84,200	218,100
Madagascar	226,600	587,000	Victoria		83,900	217,300
Baffin	196,000	507,500	Ellesmere		75,800	196,200

LONGEST RIVERS*

	miles	kilometers
Nile, Africa	4,160	6,695
Amazon, S. America	4,150	6,679
Chang Jiang (Yangtze), Asia	3,880	6,244
Mississippi-Missouri, N. America	3,710	5,970
Yenisey-Angara, Asia	3,610	5,810
Yellow (Huang), Asia	3,590	5,778

Antarctica has no flowing rivers.

* These lists name the longest river and the major mountain range on each continent. Rivers are listed longest to shortest. Mountain ranges are listed in alphabetical order.

MAJOR MOUNTAIN RANGES*

Alps, Europe

Andes, South America

Atlas Mountains, Africa

Great Dividing Range, Australia

Himalaya, Asia

Rocky Mountains, North America

Transantarctic Mountains, Antarctica

Ural Mountains form much of the boundary between Europe and Asia.

EARTH'S EXTREMES

Hottest Place: Dallol, Danakil Depression, Ethiopia; annual average temperature: 93°F (34°C)

Coldest Place: Ridge A, Antarctica; annual average temperature: -94°F (-70°C)

Wettest Place: Mawsynram, Assam, India; annual average rainfall: 467 in (1,187 cm)

Driest Place: Atacama Desert, Chile; rainfall barely measurable

Highest Waterfall: Angel Falls, Venezuela; 3,212 ft (979 m)

Largest Hot Desert: Sahara, Africa; 3,475,000 sq mi (9,000,000 sq km)

Largest Canyon: Grand Canyon, Colorado River, Arizona, U.S.A.; 277 mi (446 km) long along the river; 600 ft (180 m) to 18 mi (29 km) wide; about 1.1 mi (1.8 km) deep

Longest Reef: Great Barrier Reef, Australia; 1,429 mi (2,300 km)

Greatest Tidal Range: Bay of Fundy, Nova Scotia, Canada; 52 ft (16 m)

Most atlases list countries with statistical information, such as area and population, so that you can make your own chart of the largest and smallest by area and by population. Although area figures seldom change (unless there is a boundary change), population figures do. Use the country index starting on page 130 to look up this information, and go to the websites listed in Chapter 6 to keep up-to-date.

The countries of North America: North America is made up of 23 independent countries. It includes Canada, the United States, Mexico, the countries of Central America, and the islands of the West Indies. Greenland is geologically a large part of North America, but it is not a country. It is a dependency of Denmark.

The countries of South America: South America is made up of 12 independent countries and one French territory, French Guiana.

The countries of Europe: Russia is usually counted as one of Europe's 49 independent countries. Although most of its land is in Asia, most of its people and its capital city (Moscow) are west of the Ural Mountains in Europe.

The countries of Africa: Africa has 54 independent countries. Most people live along the Nile and south of the Sahara.

The countries of Asia: China is the largest country located entirely in Asia and also the most populous of Asia's 48 countries.

Australia, New Zealand, and Oceania: Australia is a continent and a country. Geographers often include it and New Zealand with the islands of the south and central Pacific and call this region Oceania. Australia is the largest and most populous of the 14 independent countries in this region.

Antarctica: This is the only continent that has no independent countries and no permanent population.

TIP # 4 Master Mental Maps

Studying geographic shapes and place-names will eventually fix mental maps in your brain. You'll be able to picture not only where a place is but also what's near it, who lives there, and lots more. The ability to produce mental images of the world characterizes all Bee champions. This requires atlas and reference book use and a good understanding of map scale.

MAP SCALE makes it possible to figure out what distance on Earth's surface is represented by a given length on a map. Large-scale maps show a limited geographic area such as a neighborhood or city in great detail. The scale on such a map may be expressed as a ratio such as 1:1,500, meaning that every inch on the map represents 1,500 inches on the ground. (That's 125 feet or less than half a football field.) This allows the cartographer to include street names, parks, and creeks. A large-scale map of the United States wouldn't fit in your backpack. In fact, you'd need a dump truck!

Small-scale maps have much less detail but cover a greater geographical area, such as a state, mountain range, or continent. The scale here may read 1:5,000,000 (one inch represents five million inches on the ground—a very long crawl). This level of detail is the only way to cover a large area such as a continent or the world so that you can study it as a whole.

The next step is adding more physical and cultural depth to these mental maps. The following categories will get you started.

PHYSICAL FEATURES

Vegetation Zones, or Biomes: There are four main categories of vegetation zones: forest, grassland, desert, and tundra. Start with these and then expand your knowledge by learning about the different types of vegetation within these categories. Vegetation is closely linked to climate.

Climate Zones: Climate is the long-term average weather conditions of a place. Most climate maps show at least five different zones: tropical, dry, temperate, continental, and polar. As you build your knowledge, you will become familiar with subcategories, such as tropical wet and dry, arid and semiarid, marine west coast, and Mediterranean.

CULTURAL FEATURES

Population Density: Population density is the average number of people living in each square mile or kilometer of a place. The population density of a country is calculated by dividing its population by its area. Asia is the most densely populated continent; Australia is the least densely populated continent (excluding Antarctica). Check out your maps and see if you can figure out why!

Religion: All of the world's major religions—Christianity, Hinduism, Judaism, Buddhism, and Islam—as well as Shinto, Taoism, and Confucianism originated in Asia. They spread around the world as people migrated to new areas.

Languages: There are thousands of languages in the world, but there are only 12 major language families. Languages in the Indo-European family, which includes English, Russian, and German, are spoken over the widest geographic area. Mandarin Chinese is spoken by the most people. Can you figure out why?

ECONOMIC FEATURES

World Economy: Familiarize yourself with terms such as primary, secondary, tertiary, and quaternary, as well as developed and developing, industrialized and nonindustrialized.

Commerce: Learn the major crops, minerals, and products that countries on each continent produce and export. Then take note of major trade alliances, such as NAFTA (North American Free Trade Agreement), the EU (European Union), WTO (World Trade Organization), and OPEC (Organization of the Petroleum Exporting Countries).

Transportation: Study maps, charts, and graphs to learn about major trade routes by land, sea, and air.

Filling in your mental maps will take some time, so be patient. Find a study method that works for you and then hop to it!

#**5** Build Your Knowledge

Conquering place-names prepares you to tackle the biggest and most rewarding challenge of preparing for the Bee: learning about the world's primary physical and cultural patterns. Understanding how the world functions as an interconnected and dynamic system is what geography is all about. Studying these patterns prepares you to combine and layer more complex geographic information onto your basic mental maps. This takes time, but the rewards are great. The following suggestions are designed to help you reach this level.

COMBINE INFORMATION

Good geographers combine information from different sources to arrive at logical conclusions. They understand the basic patterns of climate, geology, vegetation, human settlement, migration, and commerce. Combining these patterns with a knowledge of regions and place-names will empower you to answer very specific questions that otherwise might have been a choice between two guesses. At the very least it will enable you to make an educated guess when you don't know the answer. The question analyses that follow explain how this works.

1. Which city recently suffered a severe earthquake, Tokyo or Omaha?
You may not recall any recent earthquakes, but you know that Tokyo is in Japan, an island country off the east coast of Asia,

along the tectonic Ring of Fire. Omaha is a city in Nebraska, a state located in the middle of the North American plate. Since more earthquakes occur around the rim of the Pacific Ocean than anywhere else, you correctly answer **Tokyo.**

2. Which is Germany's most important export crop, wheat or palm oil?
Using your mental maps, you know that Germany is a midlatitude country in western Europe. You also know that palm trees grow in warm tropical climates and that wheat grows in more temperate regions, like the American Midwest. Given Germany's location, you reason that it is more likely to have a temperate rather than tropical climate, and you correctly answer **wheat.**

LEARN PATTERNS ON THE LAND

Interpreting a landscape is very different from memorizing names on a map. Geographers use **THEMATIC MAPS** to show patterns on the land. They start with a physical or a political base map and add layers of information to show whatever geographic theme they wish to emphasize—everything from world population and energy consumption (see map opposite, top) to shark attacks and local weather predictions.

CARTOGRAMS are special kinds of thematic maps. On them, the size of a country is based on a statistic other than land area. In the cartogram shown opposite, population determines the size of each country. This is why Nigeria, Africa's most populous country, is shown much larger than Algeria, Africa's largest country in area.

THEMATIC MAP

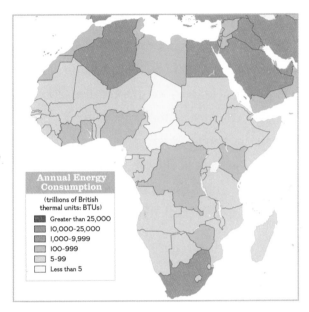

CARTOGRAM

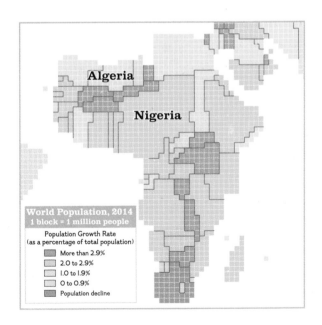

INTERPRETING GRAPHS

Graphs are another important tool that geographers use to convey information, and you can expect to encounter various kinds in the Bee. A special kind of bar graph called a population pyramid (below, top) shows the distribution of a country's population by sex and age. A more traditional style of bar graph shows the most commonly spoken languages. A climate graph (opposite page) is a combination bar and line graph that shows monthly averages of precipitation and temperature for a particular place.

POPULATION
PYRAMID

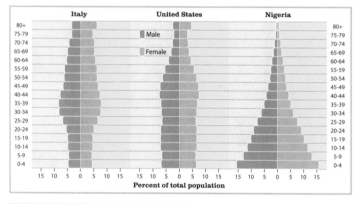

MOST
COMMONLY
SPOKEN
LANGUAGES

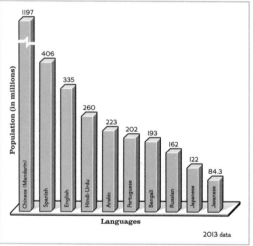

CLIMATE GRAPHS

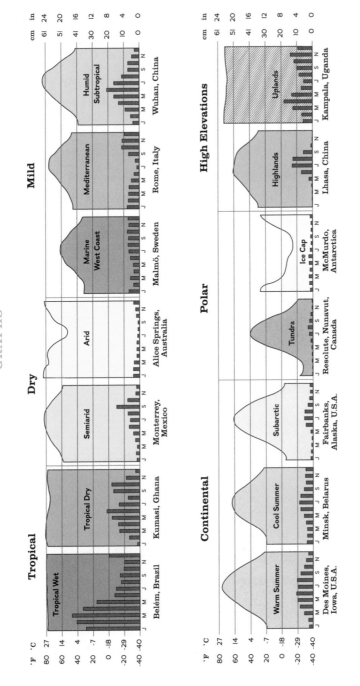

Tropical

- Tropical Wet — Belém, Brazil
- Tropical Dry — Kumasi, Ghana

Dry

- Semiarid — Monterrey, Mexico
- Arid — Alice Springs, Australia

Mild

- Marine West Coast — Malmö, Sweden
- Mediterranean — Rome, Italy
- Humid Subtropical — Wuhan, China

Continental

- Warm Summer — Des Moines, Iowa, U.S.A.
- Cool Summer — Minsk, Belarus

Polar

- Subarctic — Fairbanks, Alaska, U.S.A.
- Tundra — Resolute, Nunavut, Canada
- Ice Cap — McMurdo, Antarctica

High Elevations

- Highlands — Lhasa, China
- Uplands — Kampala, Uganda

°F: 80, 60, 40, 20, 0, -20, -40
°C: 27, 14, 4, -7, -18, -29, -40

cm: 61, 51, 41, 30, 20, 10, 0
in: 24, 20, 16, 12, 8, 4, 0

Make School Work for You

Geography is all around you! The first place to look is in school. History uniformly incorporates geography in discussing wars (the Russian winter froze the German Army in World War II), slavery (wind belts made the triangular trade possible), and ecological disasters (poor farming techniques and drought triggered the Dust Bowl during the 1930s). You will also find geography concepts in literature (Mark Twain, Robert Service, Laura Ingalls Wilder), science classes (especially Earth science and biology), mathematics (latitude and longitude, population studies, sun angles, etc.), and fine arts (dance, music, and paintings are all reflections of culture). You can even find geography in your school cafeteria (tacos, spaghetti, and rice). With good mental maps and the ability to combine information from different sources, you can spend your entire school day in excellent preparation for the Bee!

Use Your Geographic Eyes

When you can think like a geographer and understand the major patterns that influence our physical environment, culture, and economy, it's time for some field observation. The following suggestions will get your nose out of the books and into the real world.

BECOME AN OBSERVANT MALL RAT

Stores are filled with goods from every corner of the world. The origin of these products and their movement around the globe tells us much about where raw materials such as wood, minerals, and cotton come from; who makes them into finished products such as furniture, baseball bats, and shirts; and who buys them. They also furnish clues about labor use, population growth rates, and the huge difference in wealth between rich and poor countries.

Combining information from product labels and packaging with your mental maps represents advanced geographic thinking. You can practice this in stores, at school, and at home by reading the labels and packaging on products to find out where the raw materials used to make them came from and who made them.

For example, many computers are manufactured in China from European and Japanese components. They carry a U.S.A. label and are packaged in boxes made in Mexico. Most toys are manufactured in China. Much of our clothing is stitched in Mexico, Central America, or Asia. Many books are printed in Singapore. After much practice, you will find it easier to predict which country names will appear on boxes and labels. This is great evidence that your mental maps are becoming more detailed!

Check out stores that sell furniture (look for exotic woods), electronics (identify manufactured goods with components from multiple regions), and indigenous art (something that comes from everywhere). A century ago, Americans prized goods made overseas for their exotic qualities. Today, it would be extraordinarily difficult to outfit a home with products made only in North America. Global connections are the heart of the world's economy.

STOMACH MORE GEOGRAPHY

Grocery stores offer products from everywhere. Look for New Zealand kiwis, Colombian coffee, Central Asian spices, Swiss chocolate, and Mexican avocados among the zillion other products from around the world that arrive in your local food store.

Be aware that geographic place-names incorporated into product labels can sometimes lead you astray. For instance, check out fine china from Ireland, India ink bottled in South America, chile peppers grown in Mexico, English muffins baked from Nebraska wheat, and Canadian bacon from hogs raised in Iowa!

ATTEND COMMUNITY AND LOCAL EVENTS

Local communities are a great resource for learning more about your world. Keep an eye out for free concerts and lectures. Visit your museums and library display cases. If you have a college or university nearby, watch for public lectures and exhibits.

TIP # 8 Stay Current With Current Events

Current events questions query knowledge about natural disasters (floods, wildfires, tsunamis, earthquakes, volcanic eruptions, etc.), cultural and political upheaval (Libya, South Sudan, Syria, Turkey, Ukraine), international agreements (the Paris Agreement, Kyoto Protocol, Law of the Sea Treaty, Intellectual Piracy), and discoveries (archaeological finds, new plant species, energy, etc.). Almost any topic in the news, especially if it involves more than one of the categories just mentioned, is fair game for the Bee. Stories that have been the subject of recent Bee questions include the spread of AIDS, the Beijing Olympics, Iran's nuclear ambitions, and the Arab Spring.

For our purposes, we can divide current events into ongoing topics—such as climate change, immigration, and oil exploration—and breaking news stories, such as Nobel Prize announcements, international border closures, and national elections.

Your local and regional media (newspapers, TV, radio) are great ways to keep tabs on our rapidly changing world. Online news sites are also good sources, and they report events from many different perspectives. Bookmark online domestic and international newspapers so you can easily access and quickly scan them. Many of them appear in several languages, including English. They also offer great maps, photos, archived back issues, and links to related sites.

TIP # 9 Read, Read, Read

Bee champions share a passion for reading. They read books, magazines, newspapers, cereal boxes, websites—anything they can lay their eyes on. They read at school, at Grandma's, and on buses, trains, and airplanes. They read on weekends and throughout the summer. Reading helps to build your mental maps of people and places around the world. At the same time, reading becomes more geographic once you have good mental maps that enliven and enrich almost any story or news item. You can add to your mental maps as you read by keeping a map handy. Use it to find new places and features and to understand relationships between the land and the people.

TIP #10 Play Games

Chapter 6 evaluates several games that use a quiz format like the Bee's to test your knowledge of geography. The Bee website offers geography questions to give you an idea of what the questions in the contest are like.

Playing these games offers several advantages. First, they simulate the Bee by asking questions from diverse topics that require an answer in a fixed amount of time. Second, they can help you identify your weak areas so that you can concentrate on improving those skills. A final advantage is that many of these games require multiple players, which doubles the opportunity to learn, promotes discussion, and lets you benefit from the knowledge of others.

There are other kinds of fun and productive study aids. Some, such as flash cards, are helpful for testing basic facts. Others are great for gathering interesting geo-tidbits. These should be treated as supplements to your learning.

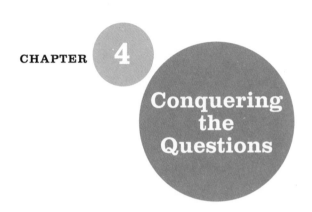

CHAPTER **4**

Conquering the Questions

This chapter presents questions that have been used at the school, state, and national levels of the Bee. Most are from the preliminary competitions, as questions there are organized by geographic categories. Samples of map, graph, and photo questions are also included.

The objective here is not *to provide questions and answers for you to memorize. Rather, it is to make you familiar with the kinds of questions asked in the Bee and show you how to look for clues within the questions that can help you come up with the right answers. Learning how to recognize the clues will reinforce the need to master the ten study tips outlined in Chapter 3. It is important to remember that the purpose of the Bee is to test your knowledge of geography. This means you don't have to worry about "trick" questions. Just take your time and think things through. Even if you answer incorrectly, you will learn something new for next time.*

Before plunging into the questions, here are a few pointers to remember about the contest. First, remember the Bee is mostly an oral competition (there are a few exceptions), so you usually won't have the benefit of seeing the questions in writing. It is important to listen carefully. The moderator will read each question only once, and you want to be sure to hear all the clues that might help you answer correctly.

Second, be sure to listen to the entire question before answering. Don't assume that you know what is going to be asked. You have only one chance to respond. Once you say your answer out loud, it cannot be taken back.

Third, don't let difficult-sounding words intimidate or sidetrack you. If the moderator trips over the pronunciation, he or she should automatically repeat the entire question. If you think having a word spelled will help you, then ask the moderator to spell it out. Just be aware that you can interrupt the competition only two times to ask to have either a question repeated or a word spelled. This rule applies to the Preliminary Competition and to the Final Round at each level of the Bee.

Finally, always speak very clearly with your best pronunciation. Don't worry if microphones are present, because they make you sound very cool and extra important!

Some Bee rounds involve questions from a single topic, such as cultural geography; others are a mix of many topics. At the school and state levels, a few rounds of questions usually offer a choice of two answers so that you have a fifty-fifty chance of answering correctly. This is to help you relax. Gradually, the questions become more difficult as you progress from round to round and from one level to the next. After all, the Bee is a contest, and ultimately only one student can be the champion. But if you stay cool, use your study tips, and look for clues, you'll be surprised at how many questions you will be able to answer correctly.

The questions that follow are organized first by the level of the Bee in which they were used and then by the round in which they appeared. Since the titles of rounds can change from year to year, and since the sample questions are taken from several different years, the titles listed here are only representative of what you might encounter. You may also notice that some questions could fit in more than one category. This overlap is just the nature of the competition. The titles of the rounds will give you a general idea of the focus of the questions included in them. The first question in each round is followed by a discussion in italics that points out clues and reminds you of the study tips that will lead you to the correct answer (in bold type). For the remaining questions in the round you are on your own. You will find the answers starting on page 125.

As you go through the questions, jot down new terms, facts, and place-names. Keep your study tools handy so you can put questions in their geographic context. Try timing yourself to get practice in answering within the 15-second time limit (12 seconds for the national Final Round questions). Since much of the Bee is an oral competition, consider having someone read the questions to you. That will teach you to listen carefully for clues. Most of all, have fun!

Round 1: State Savvy

1. Which state borders Lake Michigan—Virginia or Illinois? *You know that Lake Michigan is one of the Great Lakes, and also that Virginia borders the Atlantic Ocean, far from the Great Lakes. So you correctly answer* **Illinois.**

2. Which state has a longer border with Canada—North Dakota or Vermont?

3. Which state has a smaller population—New York or Wyoming?

4. Key West is a resort city located on an island chain that is part of which state—Rhode Island or Florida?

5. The San Andreas [sahn an-DRAY-us] Fault is located in which state—California or Washington?

6. The city of Baton Rouge [bat-un ROOHZH] is located on the Mississippi River in which state—Ohio or Louisiana?

7. The Aleutian [a-LOOH-shun] Islands are part of which state—Hawaii or Alaska?

8. Which state is the leading producer of oil and natural gas—Texas or Missouri?

9. Lexington and Bowling Green are cities located in which state—Kentucky or Delaware?

10. Which state is located in the Great Plains—Kansas or Oregon?

Round 2: U.S. Road Trip

1. To which state would you travel to visit Gettysburg and also watch the Pirates play baseball in Pittsburgh—Iowa or Pennsylvania? *Even if you are not sure about Gettysburg or you are not a fan of baseball, the main clue here is the major city of Pittsburgh, which you know is in* **Pennsylvania.**

2. To visit a desert museum in Tucson [TOOH-sahn] or hike the red rocks of Sedona, you would travel to which state—Arizona or Utah?

3. Which state would you visit to ride the Ferris wheel on Navy Pier and see President Abraham Lincoln's home in Springfield—Illinois or Nebraska?

4. To stroll the San Antonio River Walk or watch the Cowboys play football near Dallas, you would travel to which state—Montana or Texas?

5. Which state would you visit to swim in the Lake of the Ozarks and climb the Gateway Arch in St. Louis—Oklahoma or Missouri?

6. To which state would you travel to visit historic Mount Vernon and explore caverns in the Shenandoah Valley—Rhode Island or Virginia?

7. To visit Jackson Hole and climb Devils Tower, you would travel to which state—North Dakota or Wyoming?

8. To visit Seneca Caverns in the Allegheny Mountains and tour a restored coal mine in Beckley, you would travel to which state—West Virginia or Iowa?

9. If you wanted to visit Mount St. Helens National Volcanic Monument and go sailing on Puget [PYOO-jet] Sound, you would travel to which state—Washington or South Dakota?

10. The city of Nashville, located on the Cumberland River, is home to the Grand Ole Opry in which state—Tennessee or Kentucky?

Round 3: Discover National Parks

1. Visitors to Channel Islands National Park in California can take a boat tour to see which animal—penguin or gray whale? *Using your knowledge of animals, you know that penguins live in a cold environment, but coastal California has a mild climate. Therefore, you correctly answer the* **gray whale.**

2. Visitors to Voyageurs National Park in Minnesota can hike through what kind of vegetation—spruce trees or cacti?

3. Which animal roams the high mountain meadows of Olympic National Park in Washington—elk or jaguar?

4. At dusk in summer, visitors to Carlsbad Caverns National Park in New Mexico can watch thousands of which animal fly from the cave—cardinals or bats?

5. Which climate type is found in Denali National Park and Preserve in Alaska—subarctic or tropical wet?

6. Visitors to Biscayne National Park in Florida can go fishing and lobstering along the shore of which kind of habitat—mangrove or desert?

7. Which animal roams the slopes of Lassen Volcanic National Park in California—black bear or polar bear?

8. The tide pools at Acadia National Park in Maine are home to which animal—sea star or giant squid?

9. Yellowstone National Park in the western United States is home to the world's largest collection of which geothermal feature—geyser or glacier?

10. Visitors to Congaree [KAHN-guh-ree] National Park in South Carolina can paddle a canoe past which kind of vegetation— arctic moss or bald cypress?

Round 4: Weird But True!

1. In France, ketchup is banned in elementary schools. It's weird but true! France is located on which continent that borders the Bay of Biscay? *Not sure about the Bay of Biscay? Close your eyes and draw on your mental map of the world. Where is France? Yes, you remember it is a country in western* **Europe.**

2. In Singapore, chewing gum is only available with a prescription. It's weird but true! Singapore is part of which continent that is crossed by the Mekong River?

3. A koala sleeps for up to 22 hours a day. It's weird but true! Koalas live in the states of Queensland and New South Wales on which continent?

4. In Morocco, goats climb trees to get their favorite fruit. It's weird but true! Morocco is located on which continent that includes the Atlas Mountains?

5. Of all new cars sold in Brazil, 90 percent use fuel made from sugarcane. It's weird but true! Brazil is located on which continent that borders the Caribbean Sea?

6. The numbers we write with today were invented in India 2,000 years ago. It's weird but true! India is located on which continent that borders the Arabian Sea?

7. More earthquakes occur in Alaska than in any other U.S. state. It's weird but true! Alaska is located on which continent that borders Hudson Bay?

8. Elephants can swim for up to six hours without resting. It's weird but true! Elephants can be found in Tanzania and Zambia on which continent?

9. You can ride a Ferris wheel underground in Romania. It's weird but true! Romania is located on which continent that is crossed by the Danube River?

10. Surgeons sometimes use sea coral to replace human bone. It's weird but true! The world's largest coral reef system, the Great Barrier Reef, is located off the coast of which continent?

Round 5: Geo Extremes

1. Some of the world's tallest mountains are located in which Asian country—Israel or Nepal? *It's time for your mental map again. Visualize the location of Israel—a relatively flat, dry country on the eastern shore of the Mediterranean Sea—so you correctly answer* **Nepal.**

2. Which country is Africa's largest by area—Algeria or Malawi [ma-LAH-wee]?

3. The world's largest salt flat is located in the Altiplano region in which country—Guatemala or Bolivia?

4. Which country is one of the leading producers of oil in the world—the United States or Oman?

5. The world's longest road tunnel is located northeast of Bergen in which Scandinavian country—Italy or Norway?

6. The world's hottest inhabited place, with a record high annual average temperature of 93 degrees, is located near Eritrea [er-ih-TREE-ah] in which country—Ethiopia or Croatia?

7. Which is Africa's most populous country—Nigeria or Sudan?

8. Which landlocked country is located farther from an ocean—Paraguay or Kazakhstan?

9. Tugela [too-gay-luh] Falls, the highest waterfall in Africa, is located near the border between Lesotho [leh-soo-too] and which other country—Eritrea or South Africa?

10. What is the largest island by area in the Caribbean Sea—Cuba or Jamaica?

Round 6: Odd One Out

1. Which country is not crossed by the Tropic of Capricorn—Brazil, Egypt, or Australia? *You need to take this question apart to arrive at the answer. You know that the Tropic of Capricorn is south of the Equator. Your mental map tells you that Australia and much of Brazil lie south of the Equator, so they must be the ones crossed by the Tropic of Capricorn, and* **Egypt** *is the odd one out.*

2. Which country does not border the Indian Ocean—Tanzania, Indonesia, or Uzbekistan?

3. Which country is not mostly Christian—Italy, Pakistan, or Brazil?

4. Which country is not made up of a group of islands—Japan, Thailand, or the Philippines?

5. Which country does not border Lake Victoria—Tanzania, Uganda, or Nigeria?

6. Which country does not have a border along the Red Sea—Egypt, Syria, or Eritrea?

7. Which country does not share a border with Panama—Costa Rica, Nicaragua, or Colombia?

8. Which country does not border the Adriatic Sea—Germany, Italy, or Croatia?

9. Which country is not located near the Tsushima [TSOO-SHEE-MAH] Current—Japan, South Korea, or Indonesia?

10. Which country does not include an area of humid subtropical climate—China, Uruguay, or Chad?

Round 7: Awesome Adventures

1. You can whiz along one of the world's longest series of zip lines in the Snowdonia Mountains in Wales in which European country? *You don't know where the Snowdonia Mountains are? Not a problem! You know that Wales is a part of the* **United**

Kingdom of Great Britain and Northern Ireland, so you know the correct answer.

2. Runners travel more than 150 miles in an annual desert race called the Gobi March. This race takes place south of Mongolia in which Asian country?

3. Bicyclists enjoy paths around Lake Constance, a body of water that lies on the border between Switzerland, Germany, and which other country?

4. You can strap on a hang glider's harness and soar over the city of Rio de Janeiro in which South American country?

5. Climbers can explore the ice on the Athabasca [a-thuh-BAS-kuh] Glacier. This massive river of ice is located in the Rocky Mountains in Alberta in which country?

6. Adventurers experience eight seconds of free fall while bungee jumping into Nevis Gorge on South Island. This island is part of which country located in the South Pacific?

7. Extreme kayakers maneuver through jagged rocks and rapids on the Bashkaus River, located in Siberia in which country?

8. Climb one of the tallest sand dunes in the world in a desert that borders the Atlantic Ocean in which country south of Angola?

9. Climb one of Europe's highest peaks, Mont Blanc. This mountain is located on the border between France, Switzerland, and which other country?

10. Volunteers can feed, walk, and wash elephants at wildlife sanctuaries near Kathmandu in which small Asian country?

Tiebreaker Questions

1. Name the desert that covers much of the area between Los Angeles and Death Valley in southern California. *This question requires you to recall the location of major deserts in the United States. You remember that the Mojave and Sonoran Deserts are in Southern California, but much of the Sonoran Desert extends into Mexico, so you correctly answer* **Mojave Desert.**

2. What is another term used for lines of longitude?

3. What is the name of the channel between the Atlantic and Pacific Oceans that separates South America's mainland from Tierra del Fuego?

4. The Edwards Plateau, Brazos River, and Padre Island are all physical features found in which U.S. state?

5. In 1697, Spain ceded control of what is now Haiti to which country?

6. What is the official language of Libya, Yemen, and Mauritania?

7. The Danube River flows for about 1,800 miles before emptying into what body of water?

8. The Ganges [GAN-jeez] Plain extends across much of the northern portion of which country?

SCHOOL-LEVEL FINAL ROUND

The questions in the final round are similar to those in the Preliminary Competition, except they are more difficult. The questions are not grouped into geographic categories. Instead, it is a good bet that each question will test your knowledge about a different geographic subject. The exception to this is the series of questions that pertains to a map, graph, or other visual aid.

1. Which state is bordered by Lake Erie and Kentucky?

2. The Great Salt Lake is located in which state that borders Idaho?

3. Corpus Christi and Houston are cities in which state that borders Oklahoma?

4. Which state that borders Connecticut is the smallest state in the United States?

5. Which state is bordered by Lake Superior and North Dakota?

6. The Yukon River flows through which state that borders Canada?

7. Syracuse and Buffalo are cities in which state that borders Pennsylvania?

8. Which state includes the Pacific islands of Oahu and Maui?

9. Stonehenge, an ancient group of standing stones, is located near Salisbury in what country?

10. The Sydney Opera House, with its distinctive roof resembling the sails of a ship, is a landmark in which country?

11. Zürich is a major banking center in which European country?

12. The St. Lawrence River flows out of the easternmost of the Great Lakes. Name this lake.

13. What berries are harvested from flooded bogs in some parts of the northern United States and Canada?

14. Saris [SAR-ees], garments made of lengths of cloth that are wrapped and draped around the body, are the traditional clothing of women in which country that borders Pakistan?

15. Gondolas floating on canals are associated with which city in northern Italy?

16. Name the largest island in the Greater Antilles.

The response for the next question is written. During the competition a piece of paper is provided for you. You will have 15 seconds to write your answer.

17. The classic film *The Wizard of Oz* features a young girl named Dorothy who experiences a powerful tornado in her home state where Topeka is the capital. In this story, Dorothy lives in which state located north of Oklahoma?

Map Questions

To answer the questions below, you will have to use the map showing the U.S. National Water Trails system on the following spread. This round tests your ability to identify U.S. states by locating the trails that exist along rivers, lakes, and other waterways around the country. During the Bee you will be given 15 seconds to study the map before answering your question.

1. Canoers paddling down the Hudson River Greenway Water Trail can see historic sites and wildlife marshes. This water trail is located in which state that borders Vermont?

2. The Black Canyon Water Trail is located along a rugged section of the Colorado River on the border between Arizona and which other state?

3. Kayakers can see crawfish and alligators along the Bayou Teche [BYE-oo TESH] Paddle Trail. This trail is located in which state that borders the Gulf of Mexico?

4. You can explore a stretch of the mighty Mississippi River near the Twin Cities by visiting the Mississippi National River and Recreation Area Water Trail. This trail is located in which state that borders North Dakota?

5. Paddlers can see marine mammals on the Kitsap Peninsula Water Trail. This trail travels through parts of Puget [PYOO-jet] Sound, located in which Pacific state?

6. The Red Rock Water Trail, located along Lake Red Rock, features rocky cliffs and bluffs. This trail is located in which state that borders Nebraska?

U.S. National Water Trails System

Bronx River Blueway

Hudson River Greenway W.T

Waccama River Blue Trail

Chattahoochee River National Recreation Area Water Trail

Island Loop Route

Okefenokee Wilderness Canoe Trail

Huron River W.T.

Alabama Scenic R.T.

Mississippi River Water Trail–Great River W.T.

Rock River W.T.

Mississippi Nat. River and Rec. Area W.T.

Red Rock W.T.

Bayou Teche Paddle Trail

Missouri National Recreational River Water Trail

Kansas River Water Trail

Black Canyon W.T.

Kitsap Peninsula W.T.

Willamette River Water Trail

(not to scale)

(not to scale)

Championship Round

1. Gray wolves were once wiped out from Yellowstone National Park, but they have made a comeback in recent years because of conservation efforts. Yellowstone National Park is located in Wyoming, Montana, and which other state?

2. In the popular Harry Potter book series by J. K. Rowling, Harry catches the train to Hogwarts at the Kings Cross station in what major European city?

Championship Tiebreaker Questions

1. Earth's coldest place, with an annual average temperature of -94°F, is located at Ridge A on which continent?

2. Name the most populous city in Siberia.

QUALIFYING TEST

The online Qualifying Test determines which students qualify for the state Bee. The 70 questions, including a set pertaining to a map, graph, or other visual aid, cover a wide variety of geographic topics. Each question offers a choice of four answers, and you must choose the answer you think is correct. Remember, the only time that you will take this test is if you are the winner of your School Bee.

1. How long does it take Earth to make one orbit around the sun?
   - ○ 1 month
   - ○ 1 day
   - ○ 1 week
   - ○ 1 year

2. Properties such as Boardwalk, Baltic Avenue, and Marvin Gardens in the classic board game Monopoly are named for places in what city known for its hotels and casinos?

   ○ Atlantic City

   ○ Las Vegas

   ○ New Orleans

   ○ Salt Lake City

3. Which device invented in 1837 by blacksmith John Deere allowed farmers to raise crops on large areas of the Midwest?

   ○ barbed wire

   ○ cotton gin

   ○ steel plow

   ○ telegraph

4. Since the industrial revolution, which environmental problem has caused chemical weathering that has damaged marble stonework on many buildings?

   ○ acid rain

   ○ desertification

   ○ greenhouse effect

   ○ ozone depletion

5. In which country is 26 percent of its population, more than in any other country, age 65 and older?

   ○ Afghanistan

   ○ India

   ○ Japan

   ○ Malaysia

6. A thick liquid gel obtained from what succulent plant is some-times used to treat burns and other skin conditions?

   O aloe
   O eucalyptus
   O indigo
   O poppies

7. What material was used to make traditional clogs worn by people in the Netherlands to keep their feet dry when walking through soggy areas?

   O felt
   O leather
   O rubber
   O wood

8. Some automobile companies are producing small numbers of fuel cell vehicles that are powered by what gas?

   O carbon dioxide
   O hydrogen
   O nitrogen
   O oxygen

9. Fruit trees in which state have been affected by citrus green-ing, a disease spread by small insects?

   O Alaska
   O Florida
   O Maine
   O Utah

10. Which route would you most likely take to travel from the Lincoln Memorial to the Jefferson Memorial?

O Potomac Parkway to Constitution Avenue

O 23rd Street to Ohio Drive

O Independence Avenue to 17th Street

O Constitution Avenue to Virginia Avenue

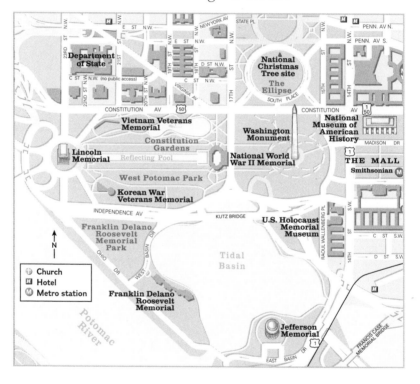

Analogies

The Qualifying Test almost always has a series of analogies in which you are asked to compare two things that have something in common. For example, in the analogy "The peso is to Mexico as the WHAT is to Japan?" the answer is yen because yen is the currency of Japan, just as the peso is the currency in Mexico. See if you can figure out the following analogies.

1. Lemurs are to Madagascar as giant tortoises are to WHAT?
   O Aleutian Islands
   O Easter Island
   O Galápagos Islands
   O Hawaiian Islands

2. Goulash is to Hungary as curry is to WHAT?
   O India
   O Japan
   O France
   O Mexico

3. Species are to animals as dialects are to WHAT?
   O languages
   O religions
   O climates
   O soils

STATE-LEVEL PRELIMINARY ROUNDS

At the state level, before the official questioning begins, there is a warm-up round to help you relax. Your answers to these questions do not count. As with the school level, the first few rounds at the state level offer a choice of answers.

Round 1: State Savvy

1. Which state has two panhandles—Iowa or West Virginia? *Close your eyes and visualize the map of the United States. You picture each state and realize that Iowa is almost box-shaped, so you correctly answer* **West Virginia.**

2. Which state is divided into parishes instead of counties—Maryland or Louisiana?

3. Which state receives more annual precipitation on average—Vermont or Utah?

4. Which state includes part of a generally flat grassland region called the High Plains—Colorado or Virginia?

5. Which state has experienced population increases from retirees seeking a warm climate—Arizona or Pennsylvania?

6. Which state borders two Canadian provinces—Maine or Idaho?

7. Which state is made up of land ceded to the United States by Mexico—Utah or Wisconsin?

8. Which state has a longer frost-free period during an average year—South Dakota or Texas?

9. The Boise River has its source in the Sawtooth Range of which state—Idaho or Ohio?

10. Trade winds contribute to the mild, tropical climate in which state—Tennessee or Hawaii?

Round 2: Our National Monuments

1. Booker T. Washington National Monument preserves the farm where this educator was born into slavery. It is located southeast of Roanoke in which state? *The question tells you Washington was born into slavery, so you know this must be a southern state. The important clue is the city of Roanoke. So use your mental map of southeastern states and correctly identify that Roanoke is in* **Virginia.**

2. Grand Portage National Monument, once an important fur-trading center, is located near both the Ontario border and Lake Superior in which present-day U.S. state?

3. Timpanogos [tim-puh-NO-guhs] Cave National Monument, containing many colorful mineral formations, is a cave system located in the Wasatch [WAH-sach] Range of which state?

4. A well-preserved fossil bed from roughly 40 million years ago can be found at John Day Fossil Beds National Monument, located near the city of Bend in which state?

5. Prehistoric mounds constructed in the shapes of mammals and birds can be found in Effigy Mounds National Monument, located northeast of Cedar Falls in which state?

6. George Washington Carver's boyhood home is preserved in the national monument bearing his name, located near Joplin in the southwestern part of which state?

7. Castle Clinton National Monument, a historic fort and now the ticketing office for ferries to Ellis Island, is located in Battery Park in which state?

8. Markers honoring both Native American warriors and members of the U.S. Army can be found at Little Bighorn Battlefield National Monument, located near Billings in which state?

9. Ancient tribes mined flint to make tools at what is now Alibates [ah-leh-BAH-tays] Flint Quarries National Monument, located north of Amarillo in which state?

10. Russell Cave National Monument protects a cave system that has evidence of human habitation beginning nearly 10,000 years ago. This monument is located northeast of Birmingham and near the Tennessee River in which southern state?

Round 3: Weird But True!

1. The heaviest cauliflower on record weighed more than a bulldog. It's weird but true! This cauliflower was grown in a greenhouse near the Pennines [PEN-nines] range in which European island country? *The question asks for an island country in Europe, so pull out your mental list of island countries to arrive at the answer. The list is short and you realize, correctly, the answer is the* **United Kingdom.**

2. The pudu [POO-doo]—a small kind of deer—runs in a zigzag pattern to escape predators. It's weird but true! This vulnerable species can be found in the Patagonia region, including the Chubut [choo-BOOT] province of which South American country?

3. One kind of mushroom resembles a human brain. It's weird but true! Brain mushrooms are poisonous but still considered a delicacy in which northern European country that includes Lake Saimaa [SAHY-mah]?

4. The coati [koh-AH-tee], a member of the raccoon family, can rotate its ankles 180 degrees. It's weird but true! The coati can be found in Chirripó National Park in the northern part of the Cordillera de Talamanca [kor-dee-YAIR-uh DAY tah-lah-MAHN-kah] in which Central American country?

5. Some old jets are placed in airplane graveyards. It's weird but true! One such airplane graveyard is located in Alice Springs, near the MacDonnell Ranges in which country?

6. The Pac-Man frog can lift three times its own body weight with its tongue. It's weird but true! This frog lives in the rain forest near Manaus [mah-NAUS] in which South American country?

7. Sputnik 1, the first satellite in space, was about the size of a beach ball. It's weird but true! This satellite was launched in 1957 from a site in what present-day country that includes Lake Balkhash [bal-KASH]?

8. The southern cassowary bird has claws nearly the length of an iPhone. It's weird but true! This bird lives on the island of Ceram [SAY-rahm] in the Maluku [mah-LOO-koo] province of which Asian country?

9. The cherimoya [cher-uh-MOY-uh] fruit, native to South America, tastes like bubble gum. It's weird but true! This fruit grows near the city of Loja [LOH-ha] in which country that borders Peru?

10. Polar bears sometimes communicate by touching noses. It's weird but true! This vulnerable species lives on the Queen Elizabeth Islands in which North American country?

Round 4: Odd Item Out

1. Which country is not landlocked—Mongolia, Nepal, or North Korea? *You know that "landlocked" means no direct access to water. Pull up that mental map again! Visualize each country and you will correctly identify* **North Korea,** *which borders water on two sides.*

2. Which country does not border Bhutan—Afghanistan, China, or India?

3. Which country does not experience a tropical wet climate—Brazil, Indonesia, or Kenya?

4. Which country does not border the Adriatic Sea—Italy, Sweden, or Albania?

5. Which country does not share a border with Bangladesh—India, Myanmar, or Vietnam?

6. Which country does not contain part of the Kalahari Desert—Tanzania, Namibia, or Botswana?

7. Which island country is not part of the Greater Antilles—Cuba, Barbados, or Jamaica?

8. In which country is ranching not a major economic activity—Italy, Australia, or the United States?

9. Which country does not have a Muslim majority—Egypt, Iran, or Russia?

10. Which country does not border the Black Sea—Georgia, Turkey, or Turkmenistan?

Round 5: Protecting Wildlife

1. The island of Java, located south of Borneo, is home to a critically endangered population of which animal—lions or rhinoceros? *You know that lions and rhinoceros once lived in Africa and Asia, but you remember that lions now live only south of the Sahara. So by elimination, one type of **rhinoceros** must be found in Java.*

2. Scientists are working to determine the economic impact of dam construction on the Mekong River system in Southeast Asia, which threatens the habitat of which animal—fin whale or river dolphin?

3. Punta Izopo is a protected area on the Caribbean coast of Honduras. This area is known for its vast mangrove forests that are home to which animal—snowy egret or chimpanzee?

4. Namibia, the first country to include environmental protection in its constitution, is home to which animal that has one of the world's longest migrations—zebra or hippo?

5. Public access is restricted in Canada's Suffield National Wildlife Area, a vast prairie grassland in Alberta that is home to which endangered animal—river otter or kangaroo rat?

6. Usually calm and nonaggressive, which animal has about half of its known population living in the Virunga [vee-RUN-gah] region of East Africa—condor or mountain gorilla?

7. Many groups are working to designate the Gulf of Corcovado, located off the southwestern coast of Chile, as a marine protected area. This area is an important feeding ground for which animal that is the largest on the planet—elephant or blue whale?

8. Wildlife groups are working to establish safe zones in New Zealand waters for which seabird that breeds only in these areas—Chatham [CHAH-tum] albatross or blue heron?

9. Cumbernauld Glen is a popular conservation area for viewing which protected animal, one of the largest remaining carnivores in Great Britain—arctic fox or badger?

10. The Sonoran Desert, which stretches across northern Mexico and the southern United States, is home to which endangered big cat—tiger or jaguar?

Round 6: Forces of Nature

1. Scientists warn that rising sea levels and decreasing freshwater resources may lead to a natural disaster in an African country where the Aswan High Dam is located. Name this country. *You know that the Aswan High Dam was built to regulate the flow of the Nile River as it passes through Egypt. Therefore, you correctly answer* **Egypt.**

2. In the summer of 2010, severe flooding left millions of people homeless, including many between the cities of Multan [mul-TAHN] and Karachi [kuh-RAH-chee] in which Asian country?

3. In 2006, Typhoon Durian caused mudslides around Mayon [mah-YAWN], a volcano on the island of Luzon. This island is part of which Asian country?

4. In 2015, a magnitude 8.3 earthquake and accompanying tsunami affected the city of Coquimbo [koh-KEEM-boh] and surrounding areas in which country that borders Argentina?

5. In 2007, flooding affected thousands of people in the central provinces of Durazno and Treinta y Tres [train-tah e trase] in South America's second smallest country by area. Name this country.

6. In 1931, an island country experienced the deadliest earthquake in its history, centered near the city of Napier on Hawke Bay. Name this country.

7. Following Hurricane Mitch in 1998, a country improved its disaster preparations and was able to reduce the damage from landslides and flooding that occurred a decade later. Name this country that borders Guatemala and Nicaragua.

8. In 2009, a plague of caterpillars destroyed crops and contaminated water supplies in a country on Africa's Atlantic coast. Name this country that borders Sierra Leone and Guinea.

9. In 2004, a tsunami destroyed many fishing operations in an island country separated from India by the Gulf of Mannar. Name this country.

10. In 1999, landslides killed tens of thousands of people north of Caracas [kah-RAH-kas] on the Caribbean coast of which South American country?

Round 7: Watery Planet
1. Which body of water is part of the Panama Canal—Lake Managua or Lake Gatún [gah-TOON]? *You remember that Managua is the capital of Nicaragua, so Lake Managua must also be in Nicaragua, and you correctly answer* **Lake Gatún.**

2. Which body of water lies north of Arnhem [ARN-hem] Land, one of the rainiest regions of Australia—Tasman Sea or Arafura [ah-rah-FOO-rah] Sea?

3. Which body of water borders Equatorial Guinea's island of Bioko [bee-OH-koh]—Gulf of Sidra or Bight of Bonny?

4. Which body of water forms an arm of the Yellow Sea—Bo Hai [HI] or Gulf of Tonkin?

5. Which body of water is known for its considerable oil and natural gas deposits—Scotia Sea or North Sea?

6. Over which body of water do many tropical storms pass on their way from the West Indies to the North American mainland—Yucatán Channel or Gulf of Guayaquil [gwi-yuh-KEEL]?

7. Which body of water is crossed by the Arctic Circle—Norwegian Sea or Baltic Sea?

8. Which body of water is located along a disputed border in West Asia—Lake Nasser or Sea of Galilee?

9. Which body of water lies southwest of the South Shetland Islands—Timor Sea or Bellingshausen [BELL-ingz-how-zen] Sea?

10. Which body of water lies west of Naples, Italy—Tyrrhenian [teh-REE-nee-en] Sea or Ionian Sea?

Round 8: World Music

1. Rap music called Rap-e [RAH-pee] Farsi sometimes critiques the government in which country south of the Caspian Sea? *Using your mental map, you know that Iran lies south of the Caspian Sea, and you recall that Farsi is a major language there. So you correctly answer* **Iran.**

2. Gamelan [GA-muh-lan] orchestras composed of gongs struck by mallets provide the music for many temple ceremonies on the island of Bali in which country?

3. Maracas, or rattles made from gourds, are important to many songs and dances in the country that includes Lake Maracaibo [mah-rah-KI-boh]. Name this country.

4. The duduk [doo-DOOK], a type of oboe traditionally made from apricot wood, is especially important in the area around the city of Yerevan [yer-eh-VAHN] in which country?

5. Bhangra [BAHN-gruh] is a syncopated kind of music played by farmers in the state of Punjab in which country that borders Nepal?

6. Vimbuza [vim-BOO-zah], which combines dances and drum music, is an important healing ritual for the Tumbuka [TOOM-boo-kah] people living in which African country formerly known as Nyasaland [NYAH-sah-land]?

7. Bomba, a form of music and dance that combines Andean guitar and rhythms from Africa, is traditional in a country that borders Peru and Colombia. Name this country.

8. Bachata [ba-SHA-ta], a style of slow romantic music, developed among the poor communities in what Caribbean country that borders Haiti?

9. Calypso music, which often has lyrics that comment on social conditions, originated in which Caribbean country southeast of Grenada [gruh-NAY-duh]?

10. Timbila [tim-BEE-luh], or wooden xylophones, are traditionally played in the Chopi [SHAH-pee] communities in which country that borders South Africa and Tanzania?

Tiebreaker Questions

1. Lake Assal [ah-SAHL], west of the Gulf of Aden, lies about 500 feet below sea level and is the lowest point on which continent? *The Gulf of Aden lies south of the Arabian Peninsula, which is part of Asia. But Lake Assal is west of the gulf and according to your mental map that means it is in Djibouti, which is in* **Africa.**

2. A ryokan [ree-oh-kun], a type of traditional inn, has been operating for nearly 1,300 years in Komatsu [koh-maht-soo]. Komatsu is on the island of Honshu in what country?

3. The European Food Safety Authority is located in the city of Parma in what country?

4. Flightless, nocturnal parrots called kakapos [ka-ka-pohs] live in island sanctuaries in the Fiordland and Stewart Island areas of what country?

5. The Falkland Islands, an overseas territory of the United Kingdom, are also claimed by Argentina. These islands are located in which major ocean?

6. The 2010 World Cup final was held at Soccer City Stadium in the most populous city in South Africa. Name this city.

7. James Bay, which borders Ontario and Quebec, is a southern extension of what body of water?

8. The Persian New Year is a national holiday in a country that includes the site of Persepolis [per-SEP-uh-lis], which was once the capital of ancient Persia. Name this present-day country.

STATE-LEVEL FINAL ROUND

The only rounds of questions organized by topics in the State Finals are those that deal with a theme or visual materials, such as maps, graphs, or photographs. The following randomly selected examples are designed to give you an idea of what you can expect for these kinds of rounds.

1. The city of Tuskegee is southeast of Lake Martin in what state that borders Georgia?

2. Manassas and Fredericksburg are Civil War battle sites in what state?

3. A state known for its Cajun culture includes the towns of Lake Charles and Lafayette. Name this state.

4. Kilauea [kee-lau-WAY-ah], an active volcano, is near the coast in the southeastern part of what state?

5. Padre Island National Seashore lies on a barrier island south of Corpus Christi in what state?

6. Santa Monica Pier, the official western end of Route 66, is in what state?

7. Buzzards Bay and Nantucket Sound border what state?

8. Sioux City and the city of Council Bluffs are close to Nebraska in what neighboring state?

9. You can eat oyaki dumplings while riding a train to the mountain city of Nagano [nah-GAH-noh] in which country?

10. Nantes [NANTS], located on the Loire [LWAHR] River, was the home of writer Jules Verne and is located in which country?

11. Arequipa [ar-uh-KEE-pah], a center for Andean textiles, is located in which country that borders Brazil?

12. Jaipur [JI-poor], known as the "pink city" due to the color of the stone used for its buildings, is located in which Asian country?

13. Lake Lucerne is located in the Alps in which European country?

14. The tropical island of Negros [NAY-grohs] borders the Sulu Sea and is part of which Asian island country?

15. Milford Sound, a fjord carved by glacial erosion, borders South Island in which Southern Hemisphere country?

16. Eucalyptus forests can be found in the state of Victoria in which country?

The response for the next question is written. During the competition a piece of paper will be provided for you. You will have 15 seconds to write your answer.

17. Recent world weather patterns have been influenced by El Niño, which is characterized by unusually warm water temperatures in which ocean?

Map Questions

To answer the questions below, you will have to use the map showing locations of National Parks. During the Bee you will be given 15 seconds to study the map and give your answer.

1. You can hike steep switchbacks on Old Rag Mountain and see dramatic views of the Blue Ridge Mountains in Shenandoah National Park. Give the number of this park and name the state.

2. In Zion National Park, located in the Colorado Plateau region, you can rappel down 100-foot cliffs and go canyoneering in the slot canyons. Give the number of this park and name the state.

3. You can kayak and fish for trout on Jackson Lake, a glacial lake located in Grand Teton National Park near Jackson Hole. Give the number of this park and name the state.

4. Visitors to Biscayne National Park can see colorful fish while snorkeling through its shallow reefs in the Atlantic Ocean. Give the number of this park and name the state.

5. Sandboarding is a popular activity in Great Sand Dunes National Park and Preserve, located in the northern part of the Sangre de Cristo Mountains. Give the number of this park and name the state.

6. You can soar in a biplane above the rocky shores of Acadia National Park, which includes Mount Desert Island. Give the number of this park and name the state.

7. Visitors can bathe in the spring waters in Hot Springs National Park, located in the Ouachita [WAH-sheh-tah] Mountains. Give the number of this park and name the state.

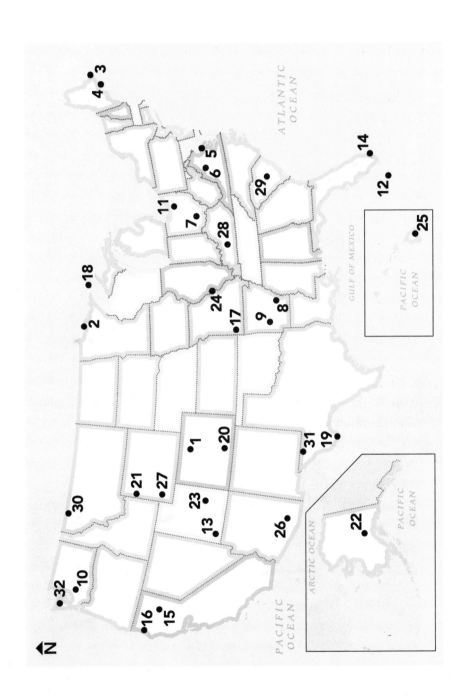

Photo Questions

1. Photographer John Stanmeyer captured Mount Bromo and Mount Semeru [seh-MER-oo] erupting simultaneously on the island of Java in which country?

2. This African penguin got up close and personal with photographer Thomas Peschak on Mercury Island. This island is located off the coast of which country that includes Walvis Bay?

3. Photographer Paul Nicklen discovered these baby arctic foxes sitting outside their den in Svalbard [SVAHL-bar], an archipelago that belongs to which Scandinavian country?

4. This tiger shark was spotted by photographer Brian Skerry off the coast of which Caribbean country in the West Indies with Nassau as its capital?

Championship Round

1. In the newest *Star Wars* movie, *The Force Awakens,* desert scenes of the fictional planet of Jakku were filmed in a country that borders both Oman and Saudi Arabia. Name this country on the Persian Gulf.

2. In 2015, scientists sent a camera into Kavachi [kuh-VAH-chee], an underwater volcano in the Pacific Ocean, and were surprised to discover two shark species inside despite the threat of eruptions. This volcano is located near the New Georgia Islands in which country?

Championship Tiebreaker Questions

1. Santa Maria Island, where Portuguese settlers planted grapes as far back as 1430, is part of what island chain?

2. What country is the only predominantly Muslim country to have a currency called the rupee?

NATIONAL-LEVEL PRELIMINARY ROUNDS

The following questions are representative of the questions and geographic categories in the National Preliminary Competition.

Round 1: Globetrotter

1. The Benue [BAYN-way] and Kaduna [KAH-doo-NAH] Rivers are major tributaries of which West African river?

2. Mount Damavand [dahm-ah-VAHND], at more than 18,000 feet, is the highest point in which West Asian country?

Round 2: Dare to Explore

1. Although he did not succeed in finding the Northwest Passage, which British explorer sailed near a large Arctic island that now bears his name—Francis Drake or William Baffin?

2. Which female British explorer traveled throughout West Africa during the late 19th century, writing two books about her experiences—Meave Leakey or Mary Kingsley?

Round 3: Rankings

1. Place these countries in order according to their literacy rates from highest to lowest: Egypt, Indonesia, Philippines.

2. Place these lakes in order according to their longitude from west to east: Lake Balaton [BAH-lah-ton], Lake Constance, Lake Ladoga [la-DOH-ga].

Round 4: Weird But True!

1. A prison in Brazil's most populous city uses geese as an alarm system—they honk at anyone roaming the grounds! Name this major city.

2. Canadians like to eat dulse [duhls], a dried red seaweed. Dulse is served in some restaurants in which major city located along the Burrard [buh-RARD] Inlet?

Round 5: Your World

1. In January 2016, a European country announced that it had produced 42 percent of its electricity from wind power in 2015, the highest proportion ever achieved by a country. Many of these wind farms are located in the Jutland [JUT-lund] region in which country?

2. In January 2016, a country that borders the Aegean Sea held its annual Camel Wrestling Championship, an ancient tradition where camels fight each other. This competition is held in Selçuk [SEL-juk] in which country?

Round 6: Destinations of a Lifetime

1. Visit the tallest pyramid in the Yucatán Peninsula in the ancient Maya city of Cobá [ko-BAH]. Cobá is located southwest of Cancún in which Mexican state?

2. An island that is part of an overseas territory of the United Kingdom is a stopping point for birds and seals crossing the South Atlantic. It is also where the explorer Ernest Shackleton is buried. Name this large island.

Round 7: Geography Rocks!

1. Which mineral is a good conductor of electricity and is named after the island of Cyprus—copper or cobalt?

2. Some rare specimens of a gem from the Dominican Republic look blue when viewed under direct sunlight but golden brown when viewed under incandescent light. Is this gem amber or kunzite [KOON-zite]?

Round 8: World National Parks (Map Questions)

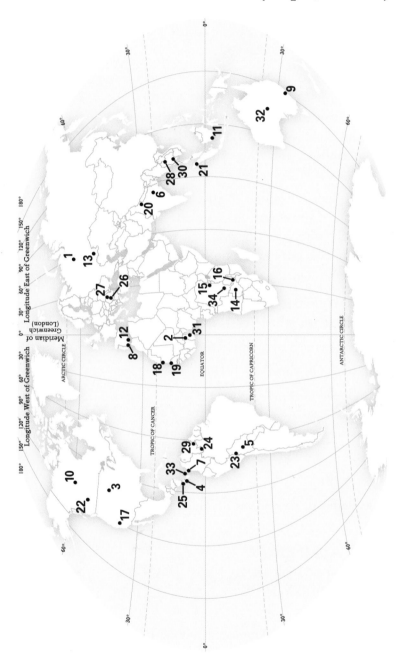

Look at the map on the previous page to give the number of the park and name the country where it is located.

1. Khao Yai [kow-yai] National Park, covering an area of more than 800 square miles and home to tropical wildlife, such as elephants and tigers, lies at the southern end of the Phetchabun [pet-chah-BOON] Range. Give the number of this park and name the country where it is located.

2. Canaima [kah-NEI-mah] National Park, covering over 11,500 square miles, is mainly located in a region called La Gran Sabana and includes the world's tallest waterfall. Give the number of this park and name the state where it is located.

Round 9: City Situation
1. Which clue correctly describes the location of Calgary, Canada?

    on the shores of Lake Ontario

    on the banks of the Bow River

    on the banks of the Red River

2. Which clue correctly describes the location of Baghdad, Iraq?

    west of Kuwait City

    west of Mosul

    on the banks of the Tigris River

Round 10: Analogies
1. Abuja [ah-BOO-jah] is to Lagos [LAH-gos] as Astana [ah-STAH-nah] is to WHAT?

2. Vesuvius is to Italy as Tajumulco [tah-hoo-MUHL-koh] is to WHAT?

GeoChallenges

At the national level, students will encounter GeoChallenges, or special questions that require critical thinking. Students will be asked to synthesize their geographic knowledge and apply it accurately, compellingly, and creatively. GeoChallenges often require an extended response in either oral or written form. The response is scored by a panel of judges based on criteria such as accuracy, reasoning, and presentation. Over time, more of these types of questions will be introduced in the Bee at all levels.

EXAMPLE:

The question below poses a real-world scenario that requires an extended oral response. After hearing the question, the student has 15 seconds to reflect, and then has 45 seconds to answer. A panel of judges will score the response based on accuracy, reasoning, and presentation.

QUESTION:

You're the owner of a riverboat cruise company that operates worldwide, and business is booming. You're looking for a popular new cruise destination. You know your customers care about a warm climate, scenery, and accessibility to the port of departure. You've narrowed the selection to three rivers: Lena River, Vistula River, and Zambezi River. Which river is the best choice for your new cruise, and why?

EXAMPLE RESPONSE:

I would choose the Zambezi River as the destination for my new riverboat cruise. It's located in the tropics, so it has a warm climate most of the year. The Lena River and Vistula River are not as warm. The Zambezi also has great scenery, with interesting wildlife along the route. And I know it's accessible because there are several major airports in the area. As a bonus, the cruise could include an excursion to Victoria Falls, one of the world's most popular tourist destinations. Overall, I think the Zambezi River is the best choice for the new cruise.

CHAPTER **5**

Tips From Bee Finalists

Use every resource you have to help your geographical journey.
—LUCY CHAE, 2015 NATIONAL TOP TEN; 2016 MASSACHUSETTS STATE RUNNER-UP

This chapter provides advice from Bee champions about the best ways to get involved in learning about geography, what to study, how to relax, and more!

Have fun! Despite what some may think, learning can be fun, especially when it involves trivia. My favorite way to study was by taking online quizzes because they helped reinforce what I knew, and made me realize what I didn't know or forgot. And the feeling of accomplishment after getting all the questions to a particularly hard quiz correct makes all the studying worth it. But more important than taking quizzes, reading books, or even looking at maps, is having the drive to learn as much as you can about the world.

Asha Jain, 2013 State Bee Champion, Wisconsin (7th Grade); 2013 Top Ten National Finalist; 2013 Team USA Member, World Championships, 1st Place; 2014 State Bee Champion, Wisconsin (8th Grade); 2014 Top Ten National Finalist

Whenever you participate in any competition, you are bound to fail at least a few times before you achieve success. This is definitely something that happened to me. When I was in fifth grade, I unfortunately missed a question during the preliminary rounds at the state level and was eliminated, even though the previous year, I had made it all the way to fourth place in my state. When you experience disappointments like this, you begin to question if studying for the Bee is even worth the time. However, if you are truly passionate about geography, you need to be able to set defeats behind you and allow them to inspire you to be better. I was able to realize that I had a passion for learning about the world and a goal to be the best. I used this failure as motivation, won my state bee the next year, and became the 2015 National Geographic Bee Runner-Up.

Shriya Yarlagadda, 2013, 2014, and 2015 State Bee Champion, Michigan (4th–6th Grade); 2015 National Runner-Up (6th Grade)

. . . .

My first tip is to definitely trust your gut ... Something that I initially struggled with during my Bee saga was impulsively changing my answers, which often deviated quite greatly from the correct answer which had been my instinct. Therefore, I adopted a policy where I always stuck to my first answer, and only ever changed it if I felt as though I had a lapse of judgment or, whilst confirming my answer, determined a flaw.

Another tip is to build a mental map. Building a mental map of a region I was being asked a question about helped me focus in on the region and develop a visual answer. For example, whenever there was a question about borders, or any question on the location of a city, state, river in relation to another landform, [a mental map] enabled me to determine the answer quite easily, as after years of compiling information, constructing a rough map of the world becomes routine.

My third and final tip is to do what works for you. While studying for the Bee, strategies will be thrown at you from all sides, and sometimes it can be overwhelming. Many times, after compiling these strategies, I would try them while being quizzed by my parents, sister, or friends, and quickly discovered what worked for me. There really is no one cookie-cutter method for winning the Bee, but the one way to find the method that you feel works best is not to just read it out of a book but to apply it in practice.

Akhil Rekulapelli, 2013–2014 State Bee Champion, Virginia (7th– 8th Grade); 2014 National Champion (8th Grade)

. . . .

It's important to study as much as you can. This also helps you feel less nervous on the competition day, because you'll feel more prepared. Taking breaks and getting some physical exercise while studying is also important and will actually help you retain the geographic information for a longer period of time.

One of the things that I struggled with was controlling my nerves during the competition. A technique I found effective was taking slow, deep breaths and focusing on my questions alone. Visualizing myself performing well also helped me to calm down. Also, don't be afraid to reach out to your parents, teachers, friends, other contestants, or even past Bee participants for advice about the competition. Think of the Bee as a team effort—everyone wants you to succeed! Lastly, forget about the competition. Geography is a fascinating and extremely relevant topic. No matter how you place in the Bee, you will have an improved knowledge of the world for the rest of your life.

Grace Rembert, 2013, 2015, and 2016 State Bee Champion; 2016 Top Ten National Finalist (8th Grade)

In my three-year history of participating in the National Geographic Bee, I have several tidbits of advice I can give to upcoming Bee participants. Although the title depicts the competition as a "Geography Bee," it is much more than just geography. The Nat Geo Bee is all about relating people, cultures, and the environment and applying them to geographical elements of certain regions around the world. When I study and prepare for the Bee, I'll scan maps with my mind, but I won't completely memorize the exact layout of a certain map. Even though I think [composing] a visualization of a map in your head is necessary for success in the Geography Bee, I think it is better to evaluate and [make] connections to the real world while analyzing maps. I also think a great study method is reading country and state indexes. These small sections of information are excellent for Bee preparation as they don't exclusively highlight geographical details. They include cultural, environmental, climate, and geopolitical information. Over the last year, the CIA *World Factbook* has become a favorite for studying.

A final tip for Geo Bee preparation is having a strong grasp of geographical reasoning. Personally, I think geographical reasoning is much more useful than memorizing geographical facts, because it challenges your mind to apply what you've learned. These are only a few of the study tips I use, but I hope they are useful in your geography preparation.
Thomas Wright, 2016 State Champion and Top Ten National Finalist (7th Grade), Wisconsin

. . . .

View the Bee as an adventure, and you, the adventurer. When adventurers discover a new place, they don't just take a quick glance and move on. Instead, they look for something interesting, and spend time to learn more about it. Similarly, when learning about a new place, don't be shy to stray away from the major facts. If you find a certain fact intriguing, read more about it, until you are satisfied with what you have learned. I found that often it was the information that I learned in these digressions that made me successful at competition.

Vansh Jain, 2009, 2010, and 2012 State Bee Champion, Wisconsin; 2009 Top Ten National Finalist (5th Grade); 2010 Top Ten National Finalist (6th Grade); 2012 Second Place National Bee (8th Grade); Three-time Top Ten National Finalist

. . . .

Two items were crucial in my Bee preparation: a small atlas and my phone. I always glanced at my atlas after finishing my work at school; constant reinforcement of your mental map is beneficial. Also, I always had oodles of geography-related Wikipedia articles open on my phone's Internet browser. I could read about exports of Zambia anytime on the bus ride home! These small things throughout my day really added up.

Most importantly, look up the things you don't know. If you hear something and don't know where it is located, take the opportunity to learn. I don't think we appreciate the Internet enough—basically everything is available. But don't turn your back on good old paper maps! Use every resource you have to help your geographical journey.

Lucy Chae, 2015 State Bee Champion, Massachusetts (7th Grade); 2015 Top Ten National Finalist; 2016 Massachusetts State Runner-Up (8th Grade)

. . . .

I prepared for the Bee by having my family go through questions in the *National Geographic Bee Official Study Guide, Afghanistan to Zimbabwe,* and *The Geography Bee Complete Preparation Handbook,* looking at atlases, and watching TV programs, especially the History and Travel

Channels. Before the competition, I contacted the previous state winner for New Jersey to see what tips he had.

Evan Meltzer, 2006 State Bee Champion, New Jersey (8th Grade)

. . . .

When preparing for the Bee, remember that the competition is not just about memorization: It requires an in-depth understanding of the United States and the world. While memorizing capitals will help with some questions, one of the best ways to prepare is by looking through maps and atlases and gaining a general idea of what places look like spatially. Preparing this way allows you to think spatially in the competition, which is something that helped me succeed. Additionally, keep in mind that while there is a time limit for answering questions, you can significantly benefit from taking your time on each one. Once you hear a question, think of an answer, confirm it mentally, and then say it aloud. Fifteen seconds is plenty of time to think about the question, so don't answer in the first one or two seconds. Also, if you can't understand a question clearly, don't hesitate to ask for a spelling or repetition. If you think it could make the difference between a right and wrong answer, it is in your best interest to use this option. Taking advantage of the time and options you have when answering a question can help you minimize mistakes and give you a competitive advantage.

Pranit Nanda, 2011 State Bee Runner-Up (5th Grade), 2012 State Bee Champion (6th Grade), Colorado; 2013 Top Ten National Finalist (7th Grade); 2014 Top Ten National Finalist (8th Grade)

. . . .

My first and most important tip is to be passionate! When preparing for the Bee, it's so important to find the aspects of geography that you're most curious about. Personally, my favorite part about geography was discovering all the unique and beautiful cultures across the globe. By learning about cultures, I was able to integrate other aspects of geography into my study routine by exploring where these cultural and ethnic groups lived, how they lived, who they interacted with, etc. Since all aspects of geography are interconnected, finding something you love to study will make it easier and more interesting to learn new things.

My second piece of advice is to just have fun with it. While that sounds clichéd, finding new and exciting ways to study is really what helped me become immersed in geography, which ultimately made me compete better. During my spring vacation between Nationals and States, my whole family would have a "multicultural week," when we would go out to a new ethnic restaurant each night and watch foreign films as I learned about various regions of the world. By doing this, I got to truly understand the places I was learning about, and even discovered my favorite international cuisine (Thai) and movie (*North Face*, a German film that I highly recommend). Also, be sure to keep up with current events by watching the news. It's the best way not only to be an informed global citizen, but also to understand where and why global issues are occurring.

Neelam Sandhu, 2012–2013 State Bee Champion, New Hampshire (7th–8th Grade); 2012–2013 Top Ten National Finalist (7th–8th Grade); 2013 National Geographic World Geography Champion (Team), St. Petersburg, Russia (8th Grade)

. . . .

There are a few tips I would like to share with all future aspirants. One is that it's never too late to start the journey of geography. If you put [in] a lot of effort and hard work, then success could come. Second, is to never get intimidated by the older folks, always believe in yourself and have confidence, but at the same time don't be overconfident. Third, if you are [made] nervous by the audience, then I recommend you look down or concentrate on a spot in the room and listen to the question, or close your eyes.

Another tip is to never blurt out the answer to a question; always process it in your mind and then give your firm answer. If you don't know the question, there will always be clues, which you can connect or relate to a certain country or place. Lastly, if you are a beginner in the Nat Geo Bee, I would prefer starting with basic facts, like U.S. states and features and at least the currency, capital, and major geographic features. A start is to have a large world wall map. Best wishes to you all geo explorers!

Ameya Mujumdar, Florida, 2014 National Runner-Up (5th Grade)

. . . .

Studying geography for me meant studying maps, first identifying all the major physical features and then, one by one, studying each of those features more closely to understand the details surrounding them ... start studying first with simple maps like [the] *National Geographic Kids Atlas*, and as you get more comfortable you can graduate to [a] more comprehensive atlas. Studying should be done starting with the simplest things and then adding layers upon that foundation. Keep a Word document for the facts so you can revise old information while also adding new facts. Whenever [you are] studying, find some fun facts about different countries, which helps to make studying interesting. Use blank maps and make sure you get a mental map of various features and locations. Sometimes the amount of material that needs to be covered seems difficult and also frustrating, so keep a mark of your progress which will help in those situations. Just remember all the studying improves your knowledge and makes you better aware of the world around [you]. That in itself is the reward you get from geography. In addition, you will know what it feels like to succeed through hard work and preparation.

Saketh Jonnalagadda, 2016 National Runner-Up (6th Grade)

CHAPTER **6**

Resources Genghis Khan Would Have Loved

By looking at maps and atlases, I was able to discover places in every corner of the world and learn enough about them that I could almost visualize myself being there.
—VANSH JAIN, 2009, 2010, 2012 NATIONAL BEE TOP TEN FINALIST

Many centuries ago the great Mongol ruler Genghis Khan united his nomad tribes into a formidable army. His Golden Horde swept across the Central Asian steppe on horseback, terrorizing and plundering settlements from the Caspian Sea to the Pacific Ocean. They devastated cities, redirected rivers, and left deserts crowded with fleeing refugees. The Chinese built the Great Wall to keep the "barbarians" out, the Persians hid from them, and the Europeans fell like matchsticks. At the time of Genghis Khan's death in 1227, he controlled one of the greatest land empires the world has ever known.

Mr. Khan succeeded because, unlike the Europeans, his army did not wear heavy armor or burden itself with supply wagons that could break down. The Mongols traveled exceptionally light and fast. Their excellent use of geographic information made this possible. Mongol scouts went out months ahead of the main army, secretly gathering crucial information about terrain, vegetation, and settlements. This later assured the best routes, food for the men and ponies, and great hideaways. In a nutshell (or saddlebag), the Mongol scouts were simply the best.

Although great for the 13th century, Genghis's information was meager compared with what our current atlases, globes, and reference books can provide. Throw in television, the Internet, e-mail, and cell phones that allow instant information to flow around the globe, and you have an advantage that might have turned back even the Golden Horde.

The Mongols aside, just imagine how historic news headlines might have read if our current geographic information and communications technology had been available long ago. We might have seen: "GPS Navigation Guides Columbus to New World (film and details at 11:00)!" "Paul Revere E-Mails Alert From North Church!" "Custer's Lieutenant Faxes Map of Indian Camps." "Cell Phone Saves Captain Scott at South Pole."

The good news today is that for modest barter or a quick crusade to your local library, even ordinary peasants can obtain geographic learning materials the great Khan would have loved (and probably even killed for). An exhaustive list would make a book in itself, so this one simply highlights proven resources that will help you learn to think like a geographer.

ATLASES

Even if you're not scheming to plunder European villages, a good world atlas belongs in every ger, or yurt. This is the standard reference for Bee preparation, and it should include a full set of political, physical, and thematic maps (population, economic, climate, etc.). Also, look for country profiles, information about the oceans, plate tectonics, time zones, geographic comparisons, and more.

Our rapidly changing world alters the political landscape very quickly, so beware if your atlas is more than five years old, as some country names and boundaries may be outdated. The same is true for population figures and similar statistics. The rule of thumb is always to look for the most recent edition. Also, check to see if a less expensive paperback edition is available.

Large World Atlases

National Geographic Atlas of the World, 10th Edition. National Geographic Books, Washington, D.C., 2014.
A superb collection of political, physical, urban, regional, and ocean-floor maps; thematic maps covering topics such as climate patterns, plate tectonics, population, economic trends, and world cultures; country profiles; satellite imagery; information on temperature and rainfall; geographic comparisons; and a comprehensive index.

Midsize World Atlases

National Geographic Family Reference Atlas of the World, 4th Edition. National Geographic Books, Washington, D.C., 2015.
A comprehensive, family-friendly atlas with sections about the world, continents, oceans, and space. It includes an expansive thematic section with maps, graphs, charts, photographs, and an extensive list of geographic comparisons.

Rand McNally Goode's World Atlas, 23rd Edition. Rand McNally & Co., Skokie, IL, 2016.

A comprehensive world atlas that includes a wide variety of thematic maps, world and regional maps, geographic comparison tables, and explanations of map scale, map projections, and Earth-sun relationships.

National Geographic Collegiate Atlas of the World, 2nd Edition. National Geographic Books, Washington, D.C., 2011.

This detailed atlas features excellent world and regional maps. The many thematic maps (e.g., Health and Literacy, Defense and Conflict, Protected Lands) are a real strength.

Children's and Student World Atlases

National Geographic Student World Atlas, 4th Edition. National Geographic Kids Books, Washington, D.C., 2014. (Grades 6–10)

Packed with informative thematic maps that explore the world's physical and human systems, focusing on geology, climate, vegetation, population, economies, food, energy, and mineral resources. For each continent there are three sets of maps (physical and political, climate and precipitation, population and predominant economies) plus a photo essay. Websites are included for finding additional information and updating statistics.

National Geographic Kids World Atlas, 4th Edition (updated). National Geographic Kids Books, Washington, D.C., 2013. (Grades 3–7)

Winner of the Parents' Choice Gold Award, this atlas contains world thematic maps, photo essays, satellite images, physical and political maps of each continent, country profiles, geographic comparisons, a glossary, and a comprehensive index.

Specialty Atlases

National Geographic Concise Atlas of the World, 4th Edition. National Geographic Books, Washington, D.C., 2016.

National Geographic Global Atlas: A Comprehensive Picture of the World Today With More Than 300 New Maps, Infographics, and Illustrations. National Geographic Books, Washington, D.C., 2013.

National Geographic Kids United States Atlas, 5th Edition. National Geographic Kids Books, Washington, D.C., 2017.
Superb U.S., state, and regional maps explain the primary geographical relationships in the United States. This fifth edition features concise state profiles, photographic essays on each region and state, and thematic spreads on topics such as natural disasters, immigration, and climate change.

Atlas of Global Development: A Visual Guide to the World's Greatest Challenges, 4th Edition. World Bank Publications, Washington, D.C., 2013.
Easy-to-read world maps, tables, and graphs highlight key social, economic, and environmental data for the world's economies. Topics include infant mortality, gross domestic product, female labor, drinking water, forest cover, and CO_2 emissions.

Student Atlas of World Politics, 10th Edition. McGraw/Dushkin, New York, NY, 2012.

Emphasizes current affairs that reflect recent developments in political geography and international relations. This collection of maps and data is particularly useful for exploring the relationships between geography and world politics.

GEOGRAPHIC REFERENCE BOOKS

Merriam-Webster's Geographical Dictionary, Revised 3rd Edition. Merriam-Webster, Inc., Springfield, MA, 2007.

Provides an alphabetical listing of more than 54,000 places and features, with concise information about each plus hundreds of maps and tables.

The National Geographic Bee Ultimate Fact Book: Countries A to Z. Andrew Wojtanik. National Geographic Kids Books, Washington, D.C., 2012.

This updated book is full of facts about 195 countries that the author compiled to help him study for and win the 2004 National Geographic Bee.

National Geographic United States Encyclopedia. National Geographic Kids Books, Washington, D.C., 2015.

Organized by geographic regions, this book is packed with specially designed maps and concise essays that explore the history, climate, natural resources, and physical features of each region, each state, the District of Columbia, and the territories.

ALMANACS

The World Almanac and Book of Facts 2017. Sarah Janssen. World Almanac Books, New York, NY, 2016.

Abundant information on essential topics, such as animals, computers, inventions, movies and television, religion, and sports. This fact book includes many photographs, illustrations, and maps, along with puzzles, brainteasers, and other activities.

The World Almanac and Book of Facts 2017. Sarah Janssen. World Almanac Books, New York, NY, 2017.

A classic annual with a price that drops during the year. Crammed with global facts from farm imports to volcanic activity to baseball batting averages.

National Geographic Almanac of World History, 3rd Edition. Patricia Daniels and Stephen G. Hyslop. National Geographic Books, Washington, D.C., 2014.

Through essays, detailed maps, charts, and time lines, this book traces world history from the dawn of humanity to the 21st century.

National Geographic Kids Almanac 2017. National Geographic Kids Books, Washington, D.C., 2016.

This colorful page-turner is packed with fun-to-browse features, useful reference material, homework help developed by educators, and quirky facts. Every chapter is updated annually with new content: animal photography; cool inventions; adventure; nature; maps of the continents; hundreds of facts and figures; and fascinating stories about incredible creatures, space, vacations, and more.

GEOGRAPHY TEXTBOOKS

Fourth- through eighth-grade social studies textbooks are a great source for learning about geography. As your skills improve, check out the textbooks for more advanced levels. Don't be afraid of college textbooks. They may be more difficult to read, but if you understand geography fundamentals they offer a comprehensive and advanced tutorial on most topics. You can find these texts in bookstores, especially college and secondhand bookstores. Or surf the Internet for the best bargains (search under "used college textbooks"). College and university libraries shelve textbooks. Many state and community colleges will allow you to obtain a library card so you can borrow books. If a book was published in the last five years, check for a companion website with chapter summaries and a dizzying array of self tests.

LITERATURE

Reading nonfiction books on just about any topic—exploration, sports, survival, wars, biography, or even regional cookbooks!—can help expand your geographic knowledge. Even fiction has to have a setting, and most authors carefully research the background for their plots. This means that just about anything you read can add to your geographic knowledge.

ONLINE RESOURCES

There are many great stops on our rapidly emerging information superhighway. Beware that URL addresses change frequently. If you have trouble finding any, consult one of the popular Internet search engines, such as Google (google.com), Yahoo! (yahoo.com), and

Bing (bing.com), and simply request the site name. In any search engine, entering key words such as geography games, geography facts, or geography maps, will produce an array of sites to explore and learn about our world.

Check out the main National Geographic website— nationalgeographic.com—or one of the following:

National Geographic Bee: nationalgeographic.com/bee: a site that offers five new National Geographic Bee questions each day

UN Atlas of the Oceans: oceansatlas.org
An excellent source of readily accessible and up-to-the-minute information about oceans. Designed for government policy experts and students alike, this site provides information relevant to the sustainable development of the oceans, from basic explanations to intricate data sets.

Quintessential Instructional Archive: quia.com/shared/geography
A good flash card quiz site, with plenty of other interactive games. Navigate the pull-down menu for dozens of worthwhile activities.

World Resources Institute: wri.org
Click on Climate and Energy.

Geography: thoughtco.com/geography-4133035
This site offers free downloads and links to other geography sites, outline maps, and current events.

Population Reference Bureau: prb.org
The best source for world population, with interactive population pyramids, a quiz, recent news, country data, and links to other sites.

The CIA *World Factbook*:
cia.gov/library/publications/the-world-factbook
Downloadable maps, current information, and background data on every country.

NASA Space Place for Kids: spaceplace.nasa.gov
This site features information on Earth's surface, weather, oceans, and more. It includes games and activities.

United Nations: un.org
Full of country facts, statistics, current events, maps, and more.

Newspapers online: onlinenewspapers.com
This site features thousands of links to all of the world's news-papers and other sources of information. A great source for current events from a global perspective. Many are published in languages native to the region, but nearly every highly populated country and many regional papers offer an English edition.

Kids and Climate Change Canada: canada.ca/en/services/environ-ment/weather/climatechange/climate-action/kids-climate-change
Check out the useful resources on this page and try taking the "Kids Challenge" and taking part in the "Creative Social Media Mission."

Canadian Geographic Education: cangeoeducation.ca
Canada's top site to learn about its people and places. Offers quizzes.

National Atlas of Canada: atlas.gc.ca
Great technical information, maps, and educational materials.

California Geographical Survey World Atlas of Panoramic
Aerial Images:
californiageographicalsurvey.com/world_atlas
Test your knowledge of mountains, rivers, peninsulas, and all the
rest—from space! Accurate and downloadable, these images offer a
perspective very different from maps.

Google Earth: google.com/earth
Curious about what La Paz, the Nile River, or the Fedchenko
Glacier actually looks like from above? Google Earth takes you there.
First, download the free software, and then use the images to build
your mental map of the world.

GREAT GEO GAMES

Carmen Sandiego. The Learning Company.
This clever quiz game tests your geographic knowledge, from the
United States and beyond.

Brain Quest—Know the States! Game. Educational Insights,
Rancho Dominguez, CA.
An entertaining board game that teaches locations, capital cities,
American culture, and scenic features for all 50 states.

Name That Country. Educational Insights,
Rancho Dominguez, CA.
A board game that uses names, salutations, or special features on postcards to help you identify countries and capitals. The game can be played at varying levels of difficulty and tests knowledge of rivers, major cities, languages, and currencies.

Go Travel: Africa, South America. Travel by Games, Clinton, IA.
These fun card games test your knowledge of the history, geography, people, plants, animals, and problems on these continents.

GeoSafari Talking Globe. Educational Insights,
Rancho Dominguez, CA.
A talking geography quiz game and globe all in one. The 5,000-interactive-question database challenges players about their world knowledge. An advanced version offers 10,000 questions.

OTHER STUDY AIDS

Globes

Globes are available from a variety of manufacturers. Be sure to check the product date before ordering. Those produced by National Geographic can be found on the Society's website (nationalgeographic.com) or by calling 1-800-647-5463.

Magazines

National Geographic magazine, *National Geographic Kids*, *National Geographic Explorer*, *Canadian Geographic*, *Time for Kids* (TFK), and newsweeklies, such as *Time, Newsweek*, and *U.S. News & World Report*, include great articles, maps, graphs, and pictures.

Television

Programming on the National Geographic Channel, PBS (*Nature, Bill Nye the Science Guy, Kratts' Creatures*, etc.), CNN, C-SPAN, the Discovery Channel, the History Channel, and nightly news broadcasts will greatly expand your world.

Mo Rocca's *Innovation Nation* on CBS will widen your worldview by introducing you to people from all over the world who are creating innovative solutions to real problems.

CD-ROMs

The National Geographic Society, Rand McNally, GeoSafari, Hammond, and George F. Cram offer many digital versions of their world atlases, picture libraries, and other specific topics (history, world regions, exploration, etc.). Be sure to check the operating system requirements before purchasing any software.

Blank Outline Maps

Free downloads are available online from the following:
National Geographic Education:
nationalgeographic.org/education/mapping/outline-map/
Arizona Geographic Alliance: geoalliance.asu.edu/maps
Search online to locate additional blank outline maps.

Note to Teachers

Our country's future absolutely depends on our ability to see the connections between ourselves and our global neighbors.
—GILBERT M. GROSVENOR (2001), CHAIRMAN OF THE BOARD, NATIONAL GEOGRAPHIC SOCIETY

The National Geographic Society developed the National Geographic Bee in response to concern about the lack of geographic knowledge among young people in the United States. In a ten-country Gallup survey conducted for the Society in 1988 and 1989, Americans 18 to 24 (the youngest group surveyed) scored lower than their counterparts in the other nine countries. Shocked by such poor results, the National Geographic Society spearheaded a campaign to return geography to American classrooms. Since 1989, the Bee has been one of several projects designed to encourage the teaching and study of geography. With more than two million fourth through eighth graders entering each year, the Bee is one of the nation's most popular academic contests.

Some parents and even a few teachers think the Bee might resemble an orderly Trivial Pursuit contest. Indeed, kids who correctly answer questions on topics such as glacial erosion, Hinduism, location, and changing political blocks humble a new flock of adults every year. The annual assembly of teachers, parents, and media is impressed not just with what the contestants know right off the bat but also with how they methodically answer questions that at first appear to stump them. This ability to think like a geographer—to integrate physical, cultural, and economic knowledge—shines through at every level of the Bee.

Teaching young people to think like geographers provides them with a vital understanding of the connections that exist among ourselves, our global neighbors, and the physical environment that supports us all. The U.S. Congress has recognized this important role by designating geography as one of ten core academic subjects included in federal education acts that have been passed into law since 1994. Unfortunately, in the No Child Left Behind Act that was passed in 2001, geography lacks the designated funding mandates that accompany other core academic subjects. Ongoing efforts by the National Geographic Society and others seek to improve this situation so that teachers can receive the support they need to provide crucial geographic education.

The National Geographic Society also offers many forms of support to teachers who seek to enhance the geographic education they provide to students. The national K–12 geography standards, published as *Geography for Life: National Geography Standards*, 2nd Edition (2012), are a comprehensive presentation of what students should know and be able to do as the result of their educational experiences. Accompanying these voluntary national standards are *Path Toward World Literacy: A Standards-Based Guide to K–12 Geography* and the Road Map Project, which present a scope and sequence for teaching geography along with explanations and activities that assist teachers, curriculum writers, parents, and the general public to effectively integrate the geography standards into the school curriculum. The National Geography Standards have been incorporated into the curriculum frameworks of almost all of the 50 U.S. states.

In addition to the national K–12 geography standards, a Network of Alliances for Geographic Education—partnerships between university faculty and K–12 educators (nationalgeographic.org/education/programs/geography-alliances)—has chapters in most U.S. states and provides training and support for educators. Whether teaching a stand-alone geography class or wishing to incorporate geography into other subjects such as history, science, or vocational education, teachers can tap into a wealth of resources through the Geographic Alliance Network. It offers opportunities for professional development training, ready-to-use lesson plans and other teaching resources, and interaction with a community of professionals at the local school, state, and university levels who provide the mentoring, contacts, assistance, and camaraderie that help to energize the daily task of teaching.

National Geographic also offers an education site and EdNet (nationalgeographic.com/foundation/geographic_literacy.html), an online community that provides education news, resources, discussion, and much more. The education site provides links to maps, activities, and other programs for educators at National Geographic.

Contact information for schools to register for the Bee, obtain the geography standards, locate a state alliance, or obtain online geography education information appears below. These are the perfect places to receive answers to your questions and to explore the world of possibilities in geography education.

Whether you are an experienced geo-educator or a newcomer, the Bee is a sure bet to stir student interest in the "Why of Where." Running the contest is simple. The Society provides registered schools with an instruction booklet, the questions and answers, certificates, and prizes. Think of the Bee as an open door to a world of fun and productive learning.

GEOGRAPHIC SUPPORT COORDINATES

To register for the National Geographic Bee

U.S. schools with students in grades 4–8 may visit natgeobee.org starting in August to register their school for the Bee. Only a school employee can register a school. The early-bird registration fee is $100 (cost in 2016) for schools that register before mid-December, and schools can pay by check or credit card. From mid-December to mid-January, the registration fee increases to $120 (cost in 2016), and schools may pay by credit card only. For the most current information, visit natgeobee.org or e-mail ngbee@ngs.org.

For information about the Canadian Geographic Challenge go to

challenge.canadiangeographic.ca/en

To find your state geographic alliance office and for other education resources, go to

nationalgeographic.org/education

To order *Geography for Life: National Geography Standards*, go to

ncge.org/geography-for-life

To order *Path Toward World Literacy: A Standards-Based Guide to K–12 Geography*, go to

amazon.com/TOWARD-WORLD-LITERACY-STANDARDS-BASED-GEOGRAPHY/dp/0792284410

To order more copies of the fifth edition of *How to Win the National Geographic Bee: Official Study Guide* or *The National Geographic Bee Ultimate Fact Book: Countries A to Z* (by 2004 Bee winner Andrew Wojtanik) go to shop.nationalgeographic.com/category/books **or any place that books are sold.**

Answers

Round 1: State Savvy
1. Illinois
2. North Dakota
3. Wyoming
4. Florida
5. California
6. Louisiana
7. Alaska
8. Texas
9. Kentucky
10. Kansas

Round 2: U.S. Road Trip
1. Pennsylvania
2. Arizona
3. Illinois
4. Texas
5. Missouri
6. Virginia
7. Wyoming
8. West Virginia
9. Washington
10. Tennessee

Round 3: Discover National Parks
1. gray whale
2. spruce trees
3. elk
4. bats
5. subarctic
6. mangrove
7. black bear
8. sea star
9. geyser
10. bald cypress

Round 4: Weird But True!
1. Europe
2. Asia
3. Australia
4. Africa
5. South America
6. Asia
7. North America
8. Africa
9. Europe
10. Australia

Round 5: Geo Extremes
1. Nepal
2. Algeria
3. Bolivia
4. United States
5. Norway
6. Ethiopia
7. Nigeria
8. Kazakhstan
9. South Africa
10. Cuba

Round 6: Odd One Out
1. Egypt
2. Uzbekistan
3. Pakistan
4. Thailand
5. Nigeria
6. Syria
7. Nicaragua
8. Germany
9. Indonesia
10. Chad

Round 7: Awesome Adventures
1. United Kingdom
2. China
3. Austria
4. Brazil
5. Canada
6. New Zealand
7. Russia
8. Namibia
9. Italy
10. Nepal

Tiebreaker Questions
1. Mojave [mo-HAH-vee] Desert
2. meridians
3. Strait of Magellan
4. Texas
5. France
6. Arabic
7. Black Sea
8. India

SCHOOL-LEVEL FINAL
1. Ohio
2. Utah
3. Texas
4. Rhode Island
5. Minnesota
6. Alaska
7. New York
8. Hawaii
9. United Kingdom
10. Australia
11. Switzerland
12. Lake Ontario
13. cranberries
14. India
15. Venice
16. Cuba
17. Kansas

Map Questions
1. New York
2. Nevada
3. Louisiana
4. Minnesota
5. Washington
6. Iowa

Championship Round
1. Idaho
2. London

Championship Tiebreaker
1. Antarctica
2. Novosibirsk
[noh-vuh-suh-BEERSK]

1. 1 year
2. Atlantic City
3. steel plow
4. acid rain
5. Japan
6. aloe
7. wood
8. hydrogen
9. Florida
10. 23rd Street to Ohio Drive

Analogies
1. Galápagos Islands
2. India
3. languages

Round 1: State Savvy
1. West Virginia
2. Louisiana
3. Vermont
4. Colorado
5. Arizona
6. Maine
7. Utah
8. Texas
9. Idaho
10. Hawaii

Round 2: Our National Monuments
1. Virginia
2. Minnesota
3. Utah
4. Oregon
5. Iowa
6. Missouri
7. New York
8. Montana
9. Texas
10. Alabama

Round 3: Weird But True!
1. United Kingdom
2. Argentina
3. Finland
4. Costa Rica
5. Australia
6. Brazil
7. Kazakhstan
8. Indonesia
9. Ecuador
10. Canada

Round 4: Odd Item Out
1. North Korea
2. Afghanistan
3. Kenya
4. Sweden
5. Vietnam
6. Tanzania
7. Barbados
8. Italy
9. Russia
10. Turkmenistan

Round 5: Protecting Wildlife
1. rhinoceros
2. river dolphin
3. snowy egret
4. zebra
5. kangaroo rat
6. mountain gorilla
7. blue whale
8. Chatham albatross
9. badger
10. jaguar

Round 6: Forces of Nature
1. Egypt
2. Pakistan
3. Philippines
4. Chile
5. Uruguay
6. New Zealand
7. Honduras
8. Liberia
9. Sri Lanka
10. Venezuela

Round 7: Watery Planet
1. Lake Gatún
2. Arafura Sea
3. Bight of Bonny
4. Bo Hai
5. North Sea
6. Yucatán Channel
7. Norwegian Sea
8. Sea of Galilee
9. Bellingshausen Sea
10. Tyrrhenian Sea

Round 8: World Music
1. Iran
2. Indonesia
3. Venezuela
4. Armenia
5. India
6. Malawi
7. Ecuador
8. Dominican Republic
9. Trinidad and Tobago
10. Mozambique

Tiebreaker Questions
1. Africa
2. Japan
3. Italy
4. New Zealand
5. Atlantic Ocean
6. Johannesburg
7. Hudson Bay
8. Iran

STATE-LEVEL FINAL
1. Alabama
2. Virginia
3. Louisiana
4. Hawaii
5. Texas
6. California
7. Massachusetts
8. Iowa
9. Japan
10. France
11. Peru
12. India
13. Switzerland
14. Philippines
15. New Zealand
16. Australia
17. Pacific Ocean

Map Questions
1. 6, Virginia
2. 13, Utah
3. 21, Wyoming
4. 14, Florida
5. 20, Colorado
6. 4, Maine
7. 9, Arkansas

Photo Questions
1. Indonesia
2. Namibia
3. Norway
4. Bahamas

Championship Round
1. United Arab Emirates
2. Solomon Islands

Championship Tiebreaker
1. Azores
2. Pakistan

NATIONAL-LEVEL PRELIMINARY

Round 1: Globetrotter
1. Niger River
2. Iran

Round 2: Dare to Explore
1. William Baffin
2. Mary Kingsley

Round 3: Rankings
1. Philippines, Indonesia, Egypt
2. Lake Constance, Lake Balaton, Lake Ladoga

Round 4: Weird But True!
1. São Paulo
2. Vancouver

Round 5: Your World
1. Denmark
2. Turkey

Round 6: Destinations of a Lifetime
1. Quintana Roo
2. South Georgia

Round 7: Geography Rocks!
1. copper
2. amber

Round 8: World National Parks (Maps Questions)
1. 30, Thailand
2. 29, Venezuela

Round 9: City Situation
1. on the banks of the Bow River
2. on the banks of the Tigris River

Round 10: Analogies
1. Almaty
2. Guatemala

Countries of the World Index

Earth's surface is approximately 70.9% water and 29.1% land. The National Geographic Society recognizes four oceans (in order of size): Pacific, Atlantic, Indian, and Arctic; and seven continents (in order of size): Asia, Africa, North America, South America, Antarctica, Europe, and Australia (including the islands of Oceania).

The U.S. Department of State recognizes 195 independent states, as well as 72 dependent areas and territories spread across six continents. Antarctica has no permanent population. It is used for peaceful purposes only and is governed under the terms of the Antarctic Treaty System. Africa has 54 countries; Europe has 49* countries; Asia has 48* countries; North America has 23 countries; Australia/Oceania has 14 countries; and South America has 12 countries.

The world population, which is estimated to be 7,323,187,457 (July 2016),† is growing at an annual rate of 1.06%. The five most populous countries are China, India, the United States, Indonesia, and Brazil. The five least populous countries are the Holy See (Vatican City), Nauru, Tuvalu, Palau, and Monaco. More than half of the world's people live in urban areas. An estimated 7,100 languages are spoken in the world. The most widely spoken as first languages are Chinese, Spanish, English, Arabic, and Hindi. The most widely observed religions are Christianity, Islam, and Hinduism.

In the country index to follow, you will find a number next to each country name. This number corresponds with each country's location on the continent map at the beginning of each section.

*Five countries are shared by Europe and Asia: Azerbaijan, Georgia, Kazakhstan, Russia, and Turkey.

†CIA *World Factbook* (July 2016)

AFRICA

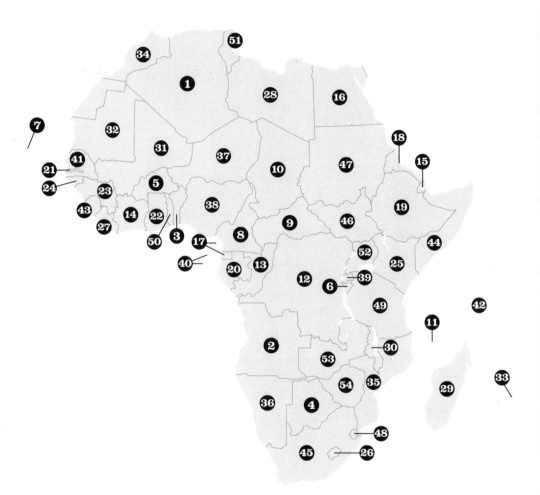

❶ ALGERIA

Area: 919,595 mi²
(2,381,740 km²)
Capital: Algiers
Population: 40,263,711
Population growth rate: 1.8%
Urban population: 70.7%
Official language: Arabic
Religion: Muslim

❷ ANGOLA

Area: 481,354 mi²
(1,246,700 km²)
Capital: Luanda
Population: 20,172,332
Population growth rate: 2.7%
Urban population: 44%
Official language: Portuguese
Religion: Christian

❸ BENIN

Area: 43,484 mi² (112,622 km²)
Capital: Porto-Novo
Population: 10,741,458
Population growth rate: 2.8%
Urban population: 44%
Official language: French
Religions: Christian, Muslim

❹ BOTSWANA

Area: 224,607 mi²
(581,730 km²)
Capital: Gaborone
Population: 2,209,208
Population growth rate: 1.2%
Urban population: 57.4%
Official language: Setswana
Religion: Christian

❺ BURKINA FASO

Area: 105,869 mi²
(274,200 km²)
Capital: Ouagadougou
Population: 19,512,533
Population growth rate: 3.0%
Urban population: 29.9%
Official language: French
Religion: Muslim

❻ BURUNDI

Area: 10,745 mi² (27,830 km²)
Capital: Bujumbura
Population: 11,099,298
Population growth rate: 3.3%
Urban population: 12.1%
Official languages: Kirundi,
French
Religion: Christian

❼ CABO VERDE

Area: 1,557 mi² (4,033 km²)
Capital: Praia
Population: 533,432
Population growth rate: 1.4%
Urban population: 65.5%
Official language: Portuguese
Religion: Christian

❽ CAMEROON

Area: 183,568 mi²
 (475,440 km²)
Capital: Yaoundé
Population: 24,360,803
Population growth rate: 2.6%
Urban population: 54.4%
Official languages: English,
 French
Religion: Christian

❾ CENTRAL AFRICAN REPUBLIC

Area: 240,535 mi²
 (622,984 km²)
Capital: Bangui
Population: 5,507,257
Population growth rate: 2.1%
Urban population: 40.0%
Official language: French
Religion: Indigenous beliefs

❿ CHAD

Area: 495,755 mi² (1,284,000 km²)
Capital: N'Djamena
Population: 11,852,462
Population growth rate: 1.9%
Urban population: 22.5%
Official languages: French,
 Arabic
Religion: Muslim

⓫ COMOROS

Area: 863 mi² (2,235 km²)
Capital: Moroni
Population: 794,678
Population growth rate: 1.7%
Urban population: 28.3%
Official languages: Arabic,
 French, Shikomoro
Religion: Muslim

⓬ CONGO, DEMOCRATIC REPUBLIC OF THE

Area: 905,355 mi² (2,344,858 km²)
Capital: Kinshasa
Population: 81,331,050
Population growth rate: 2.4%
Urban population: 42.5%
Official language: French
Religion: Christian

13 CONGO, REPUBLIC OF THE

Area: 132,047 mi²
(342,000 km²)
Capital: Brazzaville
Population: 4,852,412
Population growth rate: 2.1%
Urban population: 65.4%
Official language: French
Religion: Christian

14 CÔTE D'IVOIRE

Area: 124,504 mi²
(322,463 km²)
Capital: Yamoussoukro
Population: 23,740,424
Population growth rate: 1.9%
Urban population: 54.2%
Official language: French
Religion: Muslim

15 DJIBOUTI

Area: 8,958 mi² (23,200 km²)
Capital: Djibouti
Population: 846,687
Population growth rate: 2.2%
Urban population: 77.3%
Official languages: French,
Arabic
Religion: Muslim

16 EGYPT

Area: 386,662 mi²
(1,001,450 km²)
Capital: Cairo
Population: 94,666,993
Population growth rate: 2.5%
Urban population: 43.1%
Official language: Arabic
Religion: Muslim

17 EQUATORIAL GUINEA

Area: 10,831 mi² (28,051 km²)
Capital: Malabo
Population: 759,451
Population growth rate: 2.5%
Urban population: 39.9%
Official languages: Spanish,
French
Religion: Christian

18 ERITREA

Area: 45,406 mi² (117,600 km²)
Capital: Asmara
Population: 5,869,869
Population growth rate: 0.8%
Urban population: 22.6%
Official languages: Tigrinya,
Arabic, English
Religion: Muslim

⑲ ETHIOPIA

Area: 426,373 mi²
  (1,104,300 km²)
Capital: Addis Ababa
Population: 102,374,044
Population growth rate: 2.9%
Urban population: 19.5%
Official language: Amharic
Religion: Christian

⑳ GABON

Area: 103,347 mi²
  (267,667 km²)
Capital: Libreville
Population: 1,738,541
Population growth rate: 1.9%
Urban population: 87.2%
Official language: French
Religion: Christian

㉑ THE GAMBIA

Area: 4,363 mi² (11,300 km²)
Capital: Banjul
Population: 2,009,648
Population growth rate: 2.1%
Urban population: 59.6%
Official language: English
Religion: Muslim

㉒ GHANA

Area: 92,098 mi² (238,533 km²)
Capital: Accra
Population: 26,908,262
Population growth rate: 2.2%
Urban population: 54.0%
Official language: English
Religion: Christian

㉓ GUINEA

Area: 94,926 mi² (245,857 km²)
Capital: Conakry
Population: 12,093,349
Population growth rate: 2.6%
Urban population: 37.2%
Official language: French
Religion: Muslim

㉔ GUINEA-BISSAU

Area: 13,948 mi² (36,125 km²)
Capital: Bissau
Population: 1,759,159
Population growth rate: 1.9%
Urban population: 49.3%
Official language: Portuguese
Religion: Muslim

25 KENYA

Area: 224,081 mi² (580,367 km²)
Capital: Nairobi
Population: 46,790,758
Population growth rate: 1.8%
Urban population: 25.6%
Official languages: English, Kiswahili
Religion: Christian

26 LESOTHO

Area: 11,720 mi² (30,355 km²)
Capital: Maseru
Population: 1,953,070
Population growth rate: 0.3%
Urban population: 27.3%
Official languages: Sesotho, English
Religion: Christian

27 LIBERIA

Area: 43,000 mi² (111,369 km²)
Capital: Monrovia
Population: 4,299,944
Population growth rate: 2.4%
Urban population: 49.7%
Official language: English
Religion: Christian

28 LIBYA

Area: 679,362 mi² (1,759,540 km²)
Capital: Tripoli
Population: 6,541,948
Population growth rate: 1.8%
Urban population: 78.6%
Official language: Arabic
Religion: Muslim

29 MADAGASCAR

Area: 226,658 mi² (587,041 km²)
Capital: Antananarivo
Population: 24,430,325
Population growth rate: 2.5%
Urban population: 35.1%
Official languages: French, Malagasy
Religion: Christian

30 MALAWI

Area: 45,747 mi² (118,484 km²)
Capital: Lilongwe
Population: 18,570,321
Population growth rate: 3.3%
Urban population: 16.3%
Official languages: English, Chichewa
Religion: Christian

54

31 MALI

Area: 478,841 mi² (1,240,192 km²)
Capital: Bamako
Population: 17,467,108
Population growth rate: 3.0%
Urban population: 39.9%
Official language: French
Religion: Muslim

32 MAURITANIA

Area: 397,955 mi² (1,030,700 km²)
Capital: Nouakchott
Population: 3,677,293
Population growth rate: 2.2%
Urban population: 59.9%
Official language: Arabic
Religion: Muslim

33 MAURITIUS

Area: 788 mi² (2,040 km²)
Capital: Port Louis
Population: 1,348,242
Population growth rate: 0.6%
Urban population: 39.7%
Official languages: English, Creole
Religion: Hindu

34 MOROCCO

Area: 172,414 mi² (446,550 km²)
Capital: Rabat
Population: 33,655,786
Population growth rate: 1.0%
Urban population: 60.2%
Official language: Arabic
Religion: Muslim

35 MOZAMBIQUE

Area: 308,642 mi² (799,380 km²)
Capital: Maputo
Population: 25,930,150
Population growth rate: 2.5%
Urban population: 32.2%
Official language: Portuguese
Religion: Christian

36 NAMIBIA

Area: 318,261 mi² (824,292 km²)
Capital: Windhoek
Population: 2,436,469
Population growth rate: 2.0%
Urban population: 46.7%
Official languages: English, indigenous African languages
Religion: Christian

37 NIGER

Area: 489,191 mi²
  (1,267,000 km²)
Capital: Niamey
Population: 18,638,600
Population growth rate: 3.2%
Urban population: 18.7%
Official language: French
Religion: Muslim

38 NIGERIA

Area: 356,669 mi²
  (923,768 km²)
Capital: Abuja
Population: 186,053,386
Population growth rate: 2.4%
Urban population: 47.8%
Official language: English
Religion: Muslim

39 RWANDA

Area: 10,169 mi² (26,338 km²)
Capital: Kigali
Population: 12,988,423
Population growth rate: 2.5%
Urban population: 28.8%
Official languages:
  Kinyarwanda, French, English
Religion: Christian

40 SÃO TOMÉ AND PRÍNCIPE

Area: 372 mi² (964 km²)
Capital: São Tomé
Population: 197,541
Population growth rate: 1.8%
Urban population: 65.1%
Official language: Portuguese
Religion: Christian

41 SENEGAL

Area: 75,955 mi² (196,722 km²)
Capital: Dakar
Population: 14,320,055
Population growth rate: 2.4%
Urban population: 43.7%
Official language: French
Religion: Muslim

42 SEYCHELLES

Area: 176 mi² (455 km²)
Capital: Victoria
Population: 93,186
Population growth rate: 0.8%
Urban population: 53.9%
Official languages: Seychellois
  Creole, English, French
Religion: Christian

43 SIERRA LEONE

Area: 27,699 mi² (71,740 km²)
Capital: Freetown
Population: 6,018,888
Population growth rate: 2.4%
Urban population: 39.9%
Official language: English
Religion: Muslim

44 SOMALIA

Area: 246,201 mi² (637,657 km²)
Capital: Mogadishu
Population: 10,817,354
Population growth rate: 1.9%
Urban population: 39.6%
Official languages: Somali,
   Arabic
Religion: Muslim

45 SOUTH AFRICA

Area: 470,693 mi² (1,219,090 km²)
Capitals: Pretoria, Cape Town,
   Bloemfontein
Population: 53,300,704
Population growth rate: 1.0%
Urban population: 64.8%
Official languages: Afrikaans,
   English, indigenous African
   languages
Religion: Christian

46 SOUTH SUDAN

Area: 248,777 mi² (644,329 km²)
Capital: Juba
Population: 12,530,717
Population growth rate: 3.9%
Urban population: 18.8%
Official languages: English,
   Arabic
Religions: Christian, animist

47 SUDAN

Area: 718,723 mi²
   (1,861,484 km²)
Capital: Khartoum
Population: 36,729,501
Population growth rate: 1.7%
Urban population: 33.8%
Official languages: Arabic,
   English
Religion: Muslim

48 SWAZILAND

Area: 6,704 mi² (17,364 km²)
Capitals: Mbabane, Lobamba
Population: 1,451,428
Population growth rate: 1.1%
Urban population: 21.3%
Official languages: English,
   siSwati
Religion: Christian

49 TANZANIA

Area: 365,755 mi² (947,300 km²)
Capitals: Dodoma, Dar es Salaam
Population: 52,482,726
Population growth rate: 2.8%
Urban population: 31.6%
Official languages: Kiswahili, English
Religion: Christian

50 TOGO

Area: 21,925 mi² (56,785 km²)
Capital: Lomé
Population: 7,756,937
Population growth rate: 2.7%
Urban population: 40.0%
Official language: French
Religions: Christian, Muslim

51 TUNISIA

Area: 63,170 mi² (163,610 km²)
Capital: Tunis
Population: 11,134,588
Population growth rate: 0.9%
Urban population: 66.8%
Official language: Arabic
Religion: Muslim

52 UGANDA

Area: 93,065 mi² (241,038 km²)
Capital: Kampala
Population: 38,319,241
Population growth rate: 3.2%
Urban population: 16.1%
Official language: English
Religion: Christian

53 ZAMBIA

Area: 290,587 mi² (752,618 km²)
Capital: Lusaka
Population: 15,510,711
Population growth rate: 2.9%
Urban population: 40.9%
Official languages: English, indigenous African languages
Religion: Christian

54 ZIMBABWE

Area: 150,872 mi² (390,757 km²)
Capital: Harare
Population: 14,546,961
Population growth rate: 2.2%
Urban population: 32.4%
Official languages: Shona, Ndebele, English indigenous African languages
Religion: Christian

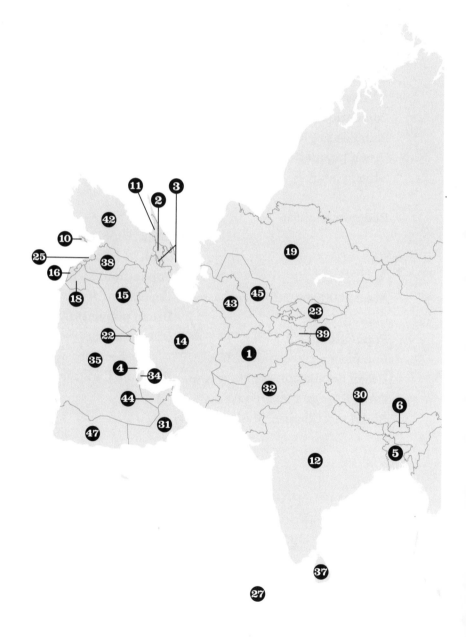

ASIA

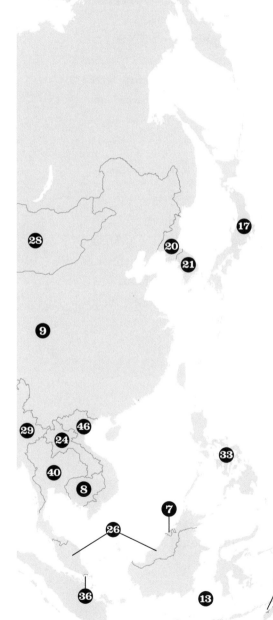

❶ AFGHANISTAN

Area: 251,827 mi²
(652,230 km²)
Capital: Kabul
Population: 33,332,025
Population growth rate: 2.3%
Urban population: 26.7%
Official languages: Dari,
Pashto
Religion: Muslim

❷ ARMENIA

Area: 11,484 mi² (29,743 km²)
Capital: Yerevan
Population: 3,051,250
Population growth rate:
–0.18%
Urban population: 62.7%
Official language: Armenian
Religion: Christian

❸ AZERBAIJAN

Area: 33,436 mi² (86,600 km²)
Capital: Baku
Population: 9,872,765
Population growth rate: 0.9%
Urban population: 54.6%
Official language: Azerbaijani
Religion: Muslim

❹ BAHRAIN

Area: 293 mi² (760 km²)
Capital: Manama
Population: 1,378,904
Population growth rate: 2.3%
Urban population: 88.8%
Official language: Arabic
Religion: Muslim

❺ BANGLADESH

Area: 57,321 mi² (148,460 km²)
Capital: Dhaka
Population: 156,186,882
Population growth rate: 1.1%
Urban population: 34.3%
Official language: Bangla
Religion: Muslim

❻ BHUTAN

Area: 14,824 mi²
(38,394 km²)
Capital: Thimphu
Population: 750,125
Population growth rate: 1.1%
Urban population: 38.6%
Official language: Dzongkha
Religion: Lamaistic Buddhist

7 BRUNEI

Area: 2,226 mi² (5,765 km²)
Capital: Bandar Seri Begawan
Population: 436,620
Population growth rate: 1.6%
Urban population: 77.2%
Official language: Malay
Religion: Muslim

8 CAMBODIA

Area: 69,898 mi² (181,035 km²)
Capital: Phnom Penh
Population: 15,957,223
Population growth rate: 1.6%
Urban population: 20.7%
Official language: Khmer
Religion: Buddhist

9 CHINA

Area: 3,705,407 mi²
(9,596,960 km²)
Capital: Beijing
Population: 1,373,541,278
Population growth rate:
0.4%
Urban population: 55.6%
Official language: Mandarin
Religions: Buddhist,
unaffiliated

10 CYPRUS

Area: 3,572 mi² (9,251 km²)
Capital: Nicosia
Population: 1,205,575
Population growth rate: 1.4%
Urban population: 66.9%
Official languages: Greek,
Turkish
Religion: Christian

11 GEORGIA

Area: 26,911 mi² (69,700 km²)
Capital: Tbilisi
Population: 4,928,052
Population growth rate:
−0.05%
Urban population: 53.6%
Official language: Georgian
Religion: Christian

12 INDIA

Area: 1,269,219 mi²
(3,287,263 km²)
Capital: New Delhi
Population: 1,266,883,598
Population growth rate: 1.2%
Urban population: 32.7%
Official language: Hindi
Religion: Hindu

13 INDONESIA

Area: 735,358 mi²
(1,904,569 km²)
Capital: Jakarta
Population: 258,316,051
Population growth rate: 0.9%
Urban population: 53.7%
Official language: Bahasa
Indonesia
Religion: Muslim

14 IRAN

Area: 636,372 mi²
(1,648,195 km²)
Capital: Tehran
Population: 82,801,633
Population growth rate: 1.2%
Urban population: 73.4%
Official language: Persian
Religion: Muslim

15 IRAQ

Area: 169,235 mi² (438,317 km²)
Capital: Baghdad
Population: 38,146,025
Population growth rate: 2.9%
Urban population: 69.5%
Official languages: Arabic,
Kurdish
Religion: Muslim

16 ISRAEL

Area: 8,019 mi² (20,770 km²)
Capitals: Jerusalem, Tel
Aviv-Yafo
Population: 8,174,527
Population growth rate: 1.5%
Urban population: 92.1%
Official language: Hebrew
Religion: Jewish

17 JAPAN

Area: 145,914 mi²
(377,915 km²)
Capital: Tokyo
Population: 126,702,133
Population growth rate: –0.19%
Urban population: 93.5%
Official language: Japanese
Religions: Shinto, Buddhist

18 JORDAN

Area: 34,495 mi² (89,342 km²)
Capital: Amman
Population: 8,185,384
Population growth rate: 0.8%
Urban population: 83.7%
Official language: Arabic
Religion: Muslim

19 KAZAKHSTAN

Area: 1,052,090 mi²
(2,724,900 km²)
Capital: Astana
Population: 18,360,353
Population growth rate: 1.1%
Urban population: 53.2%
Official languages: Kazakh,
Russian
Religion: Muslim

**20 KOREA, NORTH
(DEMOCRATIC PEOPLE'S
REPUBLIC OF)**

Area: 46,540 mi² (120,538 km²)
Capital: Pyongyang
Population: 25,115,311
Population growth rate: 0.5%
Urban population: 60.9%
Official language: Korean
Religion: None

**21 KOREA, SOUTH
(REPUBLIC OF)**

Area: 38,502 mi² (99,720 km²)
Capital: Seoul
Population: 50,924,172
Population growth rate: 0.5%
Urban population: 82.5%

Official language: Korean
Religions: Christian, Buddhist

22 KUWAIT

Area: 6,880 mi² (17,818 km²)
Capital: Kuwait City
Population: 2,832,776
Population growth rate: 1.5%
Urban population: 98.3%
Official language: Arabic
Religion: Muslim

23 KYRGYZSTAN

Area: 77,202 mi² (199,951 km²)
Capital: Bishkek
Population: 5,727,553
Population growth rate: 1.1%
Urban population: 35.7%
Official language: Kyrgyz
Religion: Muslim

24 LAOS

Area: 91,429 mi² (236,800 km²)
Capital: Vientiane
Population: 7,019,073
Population growth rate: 1.5%
Urban population: 38.6%
Official language: Lao
Religion: Buddhist

25 LEBANON
. . . .

Area: 4,015 mi² (10,400 km²)
Capital: Beirut
Population: 6,237,738
Population growth rate: 0.9%
Urban population: 87.8%
Official language: Arabic
Religions: Muslim, Christian

26 MALAYSIA
. . . .

Area: 127,355 mi²
    (329,847 km²)
Capital: Kuala Lumpur
Population: 30,949,962
Population growth rate: 1.4%
Urban population: 74.7%
Official language: Bahasa
    Malaysia
Religion: Muslim

27 MALDIVES
. . . .

Area: 115 mi² (298 km²)
Capital: Male
Population: 392,960
Population growth rate: –0.17%
Urban population: 45.5%
Official language: Dhivehi
Religion: Muslim

28 MONGOLIA
. . . .

Area: 603,909 mi²
    (1,564,116 km²)
Capital: Ulaanbaatar
Population: 3,031,330
Population growth rate: 1.3%
Urban population: 72.0%
Official language: Khalkha
    Mongol
Religion: Buddhist

29 MYANMAR (BURMA)
. . . .

Area: 261,228 mi² (676,578 km²)
Capital: Yangon (Rangoon)
Population: 56,890,418
Population growth rate: 1.0%
Urban population: 34.1%
Official language: Burmese
Religion: Buddhist

30 NEPAL
. . . .

Area: 56,827 mi² (147,181 km²)
Capital: Kathmandu
Population: 29,033,914
Population growth rate: 1.2%
Urban population: 18.6%
Official language: Nepali
Religion: Hindu

31 OMAN

Area: 119,499 mi² (309,500 km²)
Capital: Muscat
Population: 3,355,262
Population growth rate: 2.1%
Urban population: 77.6%
Official language: Arabic
Religion: Muslim

32 PAKISTAN

Area: 307,374 mi² (796,095 km²)
Capital: Islamabad
Population: 201,995,540
Population growth rate: 1.5%
Urban population: 38.8%
Official languages: Urdu, English
Religion: Muslim

33 PHILIPPINES

Area: 115,831 mi² (300,000 km²)
Capital: Manila
Population: 102,624,209
Population growth rate: 1.6%
Urban population: 44.4%
Official languages: Filipino, English
Religion: Christian

34 QATAR

Area: 4,473 mi² (11,586 km²)
Capital: Doha
Population: 2,258,283
Population growth rate: 2.6%
Urban population: 99.2%
Official language: Arabic
Religion: Muslim

35 SAUDI ARABIA

Area: 830,000 mi² (2,149,690 km²)
Capital: Riyadh
Population: 28,160,273
Population growth rate: 1.5%
Urban population: 83.1%
Official language: Arabic
Religion: Muslim

36 SINGAPORE

Area: 269 mi² (697 km²)
Capital: Singapore
Population: 5,781,728
Population growth rate: 1.9%
Urban population: 100.0%
Official languages: Mandarin, English, Malay, Tamil
Religion: Buddhist

37 SRI LANKA

Area: 25,332 mi² (65,610 km²)
Capital: Colombo
Population: 22,235,000
Population growth rate: 0.8%
Urban population: 18.4%
Official languages: Sinhala, Tamil
Religion: Buddhist

38 SYRIA

Area: 71,498 mi² (185,180 km²)
Capital: Damascus
Population: 17,185,170
Population growth rate: 1.6%
Urban population: 57.7%
Official language: Arabic
Religion: Muslim

39 TAJIKISTAN

Area: 55,637 mi² (144,100 km²)
Capital: Dushanbe
Population: 8,330,946
Population growth rate: 1.7%
Urban population: 26.8%
Official language: Tajik
Religion: Muslim

40 THAILAND

Area: 198,117 mi² (513,120 km²)
Capital: Bangkok
Population: 68,200,824
Population growth rate: 0.3%
Urban population: 50.4%
Official language: Thai
Religion: Buddhist

41 TIMOR-LESTE

Area: 5,743 mi² (14,874 km²)
Capital: Dili
Population: 1,261,072
Population growth rate: 2.4%
Urban population: 32.8%
Official languages: Tetum, Portuguese
Religion: Christian

42 TURKEY

Area: 302,535 mi² (783,562 km²)
Capital: Ankara
Population: 80,274,604
Population growth rate: 0.9%
Urban population: 73.4%
Official language: Turkish
Religion: Muslim

43 TURKMENISTAN

Area: 188,456 mi²
(488,100 km²)
Capital: Ashgabat
Population: 5,291,317
Population growth rate: 1.1%
Urban population: 50.0%
Official language: Turkmen
Religion: Muslim

44 UNITED ARAB
EMIRATES

Area: 32,278 mi² (83,600 km²)
Capital: Abu Dhabi
Population: 5,927,482
Population growth rate: 2.5%
Urban population: 85.5%
Official language: Arabic
Religion: Muslim

45 UZBEKISTAN

Area: 172,742 mi²
(447,400 km²)
Capital: Tashkent
Population: 64,430,428
Population growth rate: 0.9%
Urban population: 36.4%
Official language: Uzbek
Religion: Muslim

46 VIETNAM

Area: 127,881 mi²
(331,210 km²)
Capital: Hanoi
Population: 95,261,021
Population growth rate:
0.95%
Urban population: 33.6%
Official language: Vietnamese
Religion: Buddhist/None

47 YEMEN

Area: 203,850 mi²
(527,968 km²)
Capital: Sana'a
Population: 27,392,779
Population growth rate: 2.4%
Urban population: 34.6%
Official language: Arabic
Religion: Muslim

AUSTRALIA/
OCEANIA

❶ AUSTRALIA

Area: 2,988,902 mi²
(7,741,220 km²)
Capital: Canberra
Population: 22,992,654
Population growth rate: 1.1%
Urban population: 89.4%
Official language: English
Religion: Christian

❷ FIJI

Area: 7,056 mi² (18,274 km²)
Capital: Suva
Population: 915,303
Population growth rate: 0.6%
Urban population: 53.7%
Official languages: English,
Fijian
Religion: Christian

❸ KIRIBATI

Area: 313 mi² (811 km²)
Capital: Tarawa
Population: 106,925
Population growth rate: 1.1%
Urban population: 44.3%
Official language: English
Religion: Christian

❹ MARSHALL ISLANDS

Area: 70 mi² (181 km²)
Capital: Majuro
Population: 73,376
Population growth rate: 1.6%
Urban population: 72.7%
Official languages:
Marshallese, English
Religion: Christian

❺ MICRONESIA, FEDERATED STATES OF

Area: 271 mi² (702 km²)
Capital: Palikir
Population: 104,719
Population growth rate: –0.5%
Urban population: 22.4%
Official language: English
Religion: Christian

❻ NAURU

Area: 8 mi² (21 km²)
Capital: Yaren District (no
official capital)
Population: 9,591
Population growth rate: 0.5%
Urban population: 100.0%
Official language: Nauruan
Religion: Christian

⑦ NEW ZEALAND

Area: 103,799 mi² (268,838 km²)
Capital: Wellington
Population: 4,474,549
Population growth rate: 0.8%
Urban population: 86.3%
Official languages: English,
Maori, New Zealand Sign
Language
Religion: Christian, no religion

⑧ PALAU

Area: 177 mi² (459 km²)
Capital: Ngerulmud
Population: 21,347
Population growth rate: 0.4%
Urban population: 87.1%
Official languages: Palauan,
English
Religion: Christian

⑨ PAPUA NEW GUINEA

Area: 178,704 mi² (462,840 km²)
Capital: Port Moresby
Population: 6,791,317
Population growth rate: 1.8%
Urban population: 13.0%
Official languages: Tok Pisin,
English, Hiri Motu
Religion: Christian

⑩ SAMOA

Area: 1,093 mi² (2,831 km²)
Capital: Apia
Population: 198,926
Population growth rate: 0.6%
Urban population: 19.1%
Official language: Samoan
Religion: Christian

⑪ SOLOMON ISLANDS

Area: 11,157 mi² (28,896 km²)
Capital: Honiara
Population: 111,219
Population growth rate: 2.0%
Urban population: 22.3%
Official languages:
Melanesian pidgin, English
Religion: Christian

⑫ TONGA

Area: 288 mi² (747 km²)
Capital: Nuku'alofa
Population: 106,513
Population growth rate: –0.01%
Urban population: 23.7%
Official languages: Tongan,
English
Religion: Christian

⑬ TUVALU

Area: 10 mi² (26 km²)
Capital: Funafuti
Population: 10,959
Population growth rate: 0.9%
Urban population: 59.7%
Official languages: Tuvaluan,
  English
Religion: Christian

⑭ VANUATU

Area: 4,706 mi² (12,189 km²)
Capital: Port-Vila
Population: 277,554
Population growth rate: 1.9%
Urban population: 26.1%
Official languages: Bislama,
  English, French
Religion: Christian

EUROPE

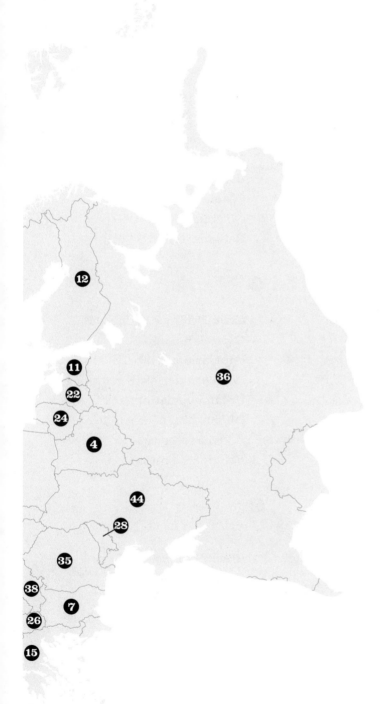

❶ ALBANIA

Area: 11,100 mi² (28,748 km²)
Capital: Tirana
Population: 3,038,594
Population growth rate: 0.3%
Urban population: 57.4%
Official language: Albanian
Religion: Muslim

❷ ANDORRA

Area: 181 mi² (468 km²)
Capital: Andorra la Vella
Population: 85,660
Population growth rate: 0.1%
Urban population: 85.1%
Official language: Catalan
Religion: Christian

❸ AUSTRIA

Area: 32,383 mi² (83,871 km²)
Capital: Vienna
Population: 8,711,770
Population growth rate: 0.5%
Urban population: 66.0%
Official language: German
Religion: Christian

❹ BELARUS

Area: 80,155 mi² (207,600 km²)
Capital: Minsk
Population: 9,570,376
Population growth rate: –0.21%
Urban population: 76.7%
Official languages: Russian, Belarusian
Religion: Christian

❺ BELGIUM

Area: 11,787 mi² (30,528 km²)
Capital: Brussels
Population: 11,409,077
Population growth rate: 0.7%
Urban population: 97.9%
Official languages: Dutch, French, German
Religion: Christian

❻ BOSNIA AND HERZEGOVINA

Area: 19,767 mi² (51,197 km²)
Capital: Sarajevo
Population: 3,861,912
Population growth rate: –0.14%
Urban population: 39.8%
Official languages: Bosnian, Serbian, Croatian
Religions: Muslim, Christian

❼ BULGARIA

Area: 42,811 mi² (110,879 km²)
Capital: Sofia
Population: 7,144,653
Population growth rate: –0.60%
Urban population: 73.9%
Official language: Bulgarian
Religion: Christian

❽ CROATIA

Area: 21,851 mi² (56,594 km²)
Capital: Zagreb
Population: 4,313,707
Population growth rate: –0.50%
Urban population: 59.0%
Official language: Croatian
Religion: Christian

❾ CZECH REPUBLIC (CZECHIA)

Area: 30,451 mi² (78,867 km²)
Capital: Prague
Population: 10,644,842
Population growth rate: 0.14%
Urban population: 73.0%
Official language: Czech
Religion: Unspecified/None

❿ DENMARK

Area: 16,639 mi² (43,094 km²)
Capital: Copenhagen
Population: 5,593,785
Population growth rate: 0.2%
Urban population: 87.7%
Official language: Danish
Religion: Christian

⓫ ESTONIA

Area: 17,463 mi² (45,228 km²)
Capital: Tallinn
Population: 1,258,545
Population growth rate: –0.54%
Urban population: 67.5%
Official language: Estonian
Religion: None

⓬ FINLAND

Area: 130,559 mi² (338,145 km²)
Capital: Helsinki
Population: 5,498,211
Population growth rate: 0.4%
Urban population: 84.2%
Official languages: Finnish, Swedish
Religion: Christian

⑬ FRANCE

Area: 212,935 mi² (551,500 km²)
Capital: Paris
Population: 66,836,154
Population growth rate: 0.4%
Urban population: 79.5%
Official language: French
Religion: Christian

⑭ GERMANY

Area: 137,847 mi²
(357,022 km²)
Capital: Berlin
Population: 23,740,424
Population growth rate: –0.16%
Urban population: 75.3%
Official language: German
Religion: Christian

⑮ GREECE

Area: 50,949 mi² (131,957 km²)
Capital: Athens
Population: 10,773,253
Population growth rate: –0.03%
Urban population: 78.0%
Official language: Greek
Religion: Christian

⑯ HOLY SEE (VATICAN CITY)

Area: 0.17 mi² (0.44 km²)
Capital: Vatican City
Population: 1,000
Population growth rate: 0.0%
Urban population: 100.0%
Official languages: Italian,
Latin, French
Religion: Christian

⑰ HUNGARY

Area: 35,918 mi²(93,028 km²)
Capital: Budapest
Population: 9,874,784
Population growth rate: –0.24%
Urban population: 71.2%
Official language: Hungarian
Religion: Christian

⑱ ICELAND

Area: 39,769 mi² (103,000 km²)
Capital: Reykjavík
Population: 335,878
Population growth rate: 1.2%
Urban population: 94.1%
Official languages: Icelandic,
English
Religion: Christian

⑲ IRELAND

Area: 27,133 mi² (70,273 km²)
Capital: Dublin
Population: 4,952,473
Population growth rate: 1.2%
Urban population: 63.2%
Official languages: English, Gaelic
Religion: Christian

⑳ ITALY

Area: 116,348 mi² (301,340 km²)
Capital: Rome
Population: 62,007,540
Population growth rate: 0.2%
Urban population: 69.0%
Official language: Italian
Religion: Christian

㉑ KOSOVO

Area: 4,203 mi² (10,887 km²)
Capital: Pristina
Population: 1,883,018
Population growth rate: N/A
Urban population: N/A
Official languages: Albanian, Serbian
Religion: Muslim

㉒ LATVIA

Area: 24,938 mi² (64,589 km²)
Capital: Riga
Population: 1,965,686
Population growth rate: –1.07%
Urban population: 67.4%
Official language: Latvian
Religion: Christian

㉓ LIECHTENSTEIN

Area: 62 mi² (160 km²)
Capital: Vaduz
Population: 37,937
Population growth rate: 0.8%
Urban population: 14.3%
Official language: German
Religion: Christian

㉔ LITHUANIA

Area: 25,212 mi² (65,300 km²)
Capital: Vilnius
Population: 2,854,235
Population growth rate: –1.06%
Urban population: 66.5%
Official language: Lithuanian
Religion: Christian

㉕ LUXEMBOURG

Area: 998 mi² (2,586 km²)
Capital: Luxembourg
Population: 582,291
Population growth rate: 2.1%
Urban population: 90.2%
Official languages:
  Luxembourgish, French,
  German
Religion: Christian

㉖ MACEDONIA

Area: 9,928 mi² (25,713 km²)
Capital: Skopje
Population: 2,100,025
Population growth rate: 0.2%
Urban population: 57.1%
Official languages:
  Macedonian, Albanian
Religion: Christian

㉗ MALTA

Area: 122 mi² (316 km²)
Capital: Valletta
Population: 415,196
Population growth rate: 0.3%
Urban population: 95.4%
Official languages: Maltese,
  English
Religion: Christian

㉘ MOLDOVA

Area: 13,070 mi² (33,851 km²)
Capital: Chisinau
Population: 3,510,485
Population growth rate: –1.04%
Urban population: 45.0%
Official language: Moldovan
Religion: Christian

㉙ MONACO

Area: 0.8 mi² (2 km²)
Capital: Monaco
Population: 30,581
Population growth rate: 0.2%
Urban population: 100.0%
Official language: French
Religion: Christian

㉚ MONTENEGRO

Area: 5,333 mi² (13,812 km²)
Capital: Podgorica
Population: 644,578
Population growth rate: –0.35%
Urban population: 64.0%
Official language:
  Montenegrin
Religion: Christian

31 NETHERLANDS

Area: 16,040 mi² (41,543 km²)
Capitals: Amsterdam, The
Hague
Population: 17,016,967
Population growth rate: 0.4%
Urban population: 90.5%
Official language: Dutch
Religion: Christian

32 NORWAY

Area: 125,021 mi² (323,802 km²)
Capital: Oslo
Population: 5,265,158
Population growth rate: 1.1%
Urban population: 80.5%
Official language: Norwegian
Religion: Christian

33 POLAND

Area: 120,728 mi²
(312,685 km²)
Capital: Warsaw
Population: 38,523,261
Population growth rate: –0.11%
Urban population: 60.5%
Official language: Polish
Religion: Christian

34 PORTUGAL

Area: 35,556 mi² (92,090 km²)
Capital: Lisbon
Population: 10,833,816
Population growth rate: 0.1%
Urban population: 63.5%
Official languages:
Portuguese, Mirandese
Religion: Christian

35 ROMANIA

Area: 92,043 mi² (238,391 km²)
Capital: Bucharest
Population: 21,599,736
Population growth rate: –0.32%
Urban population: 54.6%
Official language: Romanian
Religion: Christian

36 RUSSIA

Area: 6,601,668 mi²
(17,098,242 km²)
Capital: Moscow
Population: 142,355,415
Population growth rate: –0.06%
Urban population: 74.0%
Official language: Russian
Religions: Christian, Muslim

37 SAN MARINO

Area: 24 mi² (61 km²)
Capital: San Marino
Population: 33,285
Population growth rate: 0.8%
Urban population: 94.2%
Official language: Italian
Religion: Christian

38 SERBIA

Area: 29,913 mi² (77,474 km²)
Capital: Belgrade
Population: 7,143,921
Population growth rate: –0.46%
Urban population: 55.6%
Official language: Serbian
Religion: Christian

39 SLOVAKIA

Area: 18,933 mi² (49,035 km²)
Capital: Bratislava
Population: 5,445,802
Population growth rate: 0.01%
Urban population: 53.6%
Official language: Slovak
Religion: Christian

40 SLOVENIA

Area: 7,827 mi² (20,273 km²)
Capital: Ljubljana
Population: 1,978,029
Population growth rate: –0.29%
Urban population: 49.6%
Official language: Slovenian
Religion: Christian

41 SPAIN

Area: 195,124 mi² (505,370 km²)
Capital: Madrid
Population: 48,563,476
Population growth rate: 0.8%
Urban population: 79.6%
Official language: Castilian
    Spanish
Religion: Christian

42 SWEDEN

Area: 173,860 mi² (450,295 km²)
Capital: Stockholm
Population: 9,880,604
Population growth rate: 0.8%
Urban population: 85.8%
Official language: Swedish
Religion: Christian

④③ SWITZERLAND

Area: 15,937 mi² (41,277 km²)

Capital: Bern

Population: 8,179,294

Population growth rate: 0.7%

Urban population: 73.9%

Official languages: German,
   French, Italian, Romansch

Religion: Christian

④④ UKRAINE

Area: 233,032 mi² (603,550 km²)

Capital: Kyiv

Population: 44,209,733

Population growth rate: –0.39%

Urban population: 69.7%

Official language: Ukrainian

Religion: Christian

④⑤ UNITED KINGDOM

Area: 94,058 mi² (243,610 km²)

Capital: London

Population: 64,430,428

Population growth rate: 0.5%

Urban population: 82.6%

Official language: English

Religion: Christian

NORTH AMERICA

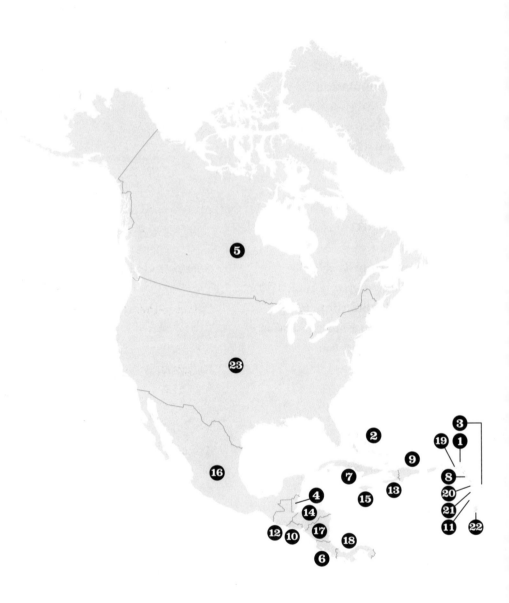

❶ ANTIGUA AND BARBUDA

Area: 171 mi² (443 km²)
Capital: Saint John's
Population: 93,581
Population growth rate: 1.2%
Urban population: 23.8%
Official language: English
Religion: Christian

❷ THE BAHAMAS

Area: 5,359 mi² (13,880 km²)
Capital: Nassau
Population: 327,316
Population growth rate: 0.8%
Urban population: 82.9%
Official language: English
Religion: Christian

❸ BARBADOS

Area: 166 mi² (430 km²)
Capital: Bridgetown
Population: 291,495
Population growth rate: 0.3%
Urban population: 31.5%
Official language: English
Religion: Christian

❹ BELIZE

Area: 8,867 mi² (22,966 km²)
Capital: Belmopan
Population: 353,858
Population growth rate: 1.8%
Urban population: 44.0%
Official language: English
Religion: Christian

❺ CANADA

Area: 3,855,103 mi²
    (9,984,670 km²)
Capital: Ottawa
Population: 35,362,905
Population growth rate: 0.7%
Urban population: 81.8%
Official languages: English,
    French
Religion: Christian

❻ COSTA RICA

Area: 19,730 mi² (51,100 km²)
Capital: San José
Population: 4,872,543
Population growth rate: 1.1%
Urban population: 38.6%
Official language: Spanish
Religion: Christian

❼ CUBA

Area: 42,803 mi² (110,860 km²)
Capital: Havana
Population: 11,179,995
Population growth rate: –0.3%
Urban population: 77.1%
Official language: Spanish
Religion: Christian

❽ DOMINICA

Area: 290 mi² (751 km²)
Capital: Roseau
Population: 15,957,223
Population growth rate: 1.6%
Urban population: 20.7%
Official language: English
Religion: Christian

❾ DOMINICAN REPUBLIC

Area: 18,792 mi² (48,670 km²)
Capital: Santo Domingo
Population: 10,606,865
Population growth rate: 1.2%
Urban population: 79.0%
Official language: Spanish
Religion: Christian

❿ EL SALVADOR

Area: 8,124 mi² (21,041 km²)
Capital: San Salvador
Population: 6,156,670
Population growth rate: 0.3%
Urban population: 66.7%
Official language: Spanish
Religion: Christian

⓫ GRENADA

Area: 133 mi² (344 km²)
Capital: Saint George's
Population: 111,219
Population growth rate: 0.5%
Urban population: 35.6%
Official language: English
Religion: Christian

⓬ GUATEMALA

Area: 42,042 mi² (108,889 km²)
Capital: Guatemala City
Population: 15,189,958
Population growth rate: 1.8%
Urban population: 51.6%
Official language: Spanish
Religion: Christian

⓭ HAITI

Area: 10,714 mi² (27,750 km²)
Capital: Port-au-Prince
Population: 10,485,800
Population growth rate: 1.7%
Urban population: 58.6%
Official languages: French,
  Creole
Religion: Christian

⓮ HONDURAS

Area: 43,278 mi² (112,090 km²)
Capital: Tegucigalpa
Population: 8,893,259
Population growth rate: 1.6%
Urban population: 54.7%
Official language: Spanish
Religion: Christian

⓯ JAMAICA

Area: 4,244 mi² (10,991 km²)
Capital: Kingston
Population: 2,970,340
Population growth rate: 0.7%
Urban population: 54.8%
Official language: English
Religion: Christian

⓰ MEXICO

Area: 758,449 mi²
  (1,964,375 km²)
Capital: Mexico City
Population: 8,174,527
Population growth rate: 1.2%
Urban population: 79.2%
Official language: Spanish
Religion: Christian

⓱ NICARAGUA

Area: 50,336 mi² (130,370 km²)
Capital: Managua
Population: 5,966,798
Population growth rate: 0.99%
Urban population: 58.8%
Official language: Spanish
Religion: Christian

⓲ PANAMA

Area: 29,120 mi² (75,420 km²)
Capital: Panama City
Population: 3,705,246
Population growth rate: 1.3%
Urban population: 66.6%
Official language: Spanish
Religion: Christian

19 SAINT KITTS AND NEVIS

Area: 101 mi² (261 km²)
Capital: Basseterre
Population: 52,329
Population growth rate: 0.8%
Urban population: 32.0%
Official language: English
Religion: Christian

20 SAINT LUCIA

Area: 238 mi² (616 km²)
Capital: Castries
Population: 164,464
Population growth rate: 0.3%
Urban population: 18.5%
Official language: English
Religion: Christian

21 SAINT VINCENT AND THE GRENADINES

Area: 150 mi² (389 km²)
Capital: Kingstown
Population: 102,350
Population growth rate: –0.3%
Urban population: 50.6%
Official language: English
Religion: Christian

22 TRINIDAD AND TOBAGO

Area: 1,980 mi² (5,128 km²)
Capital: Port of Spain
Population: 1,220,479
Population growth rate: –0.2%
Urban population: 8.4%
Official language: English
Religion: Christian

23 UNITED STATES

Area: 3,796,742 mi²
   (9,833,517 km²)
Capital: Washington, D.C.
Population: 323,995,528
Population growth rate: 0.8%
Urban population: 81.6%
Official language: English

SOUTH
AMERICA

❶ ARGENTINA

Area: 1,073,518 mi² (2,780,400 km²)

Capital: Buenos Aires

Population: 43,886,748

Population growth rate: 0.9%

Urban population: 91.8%

Official language: Spanish

Religion: Christian

❷ BOLIVIA

Area: 424,164 mi² (1,098,581 km²)

Capitals: La Paz, Sucre

Population: 10,969,649

Population growth rate: 1.5%

Urban population: 68.5%

Official languages: Spanish, Quechua, Aymara, Guarani

Religion: Christian

❸ BRAZIL

Area: 3,287,957 mi² (8,515,770 km²)

Capital: Brasilia

Population: 205,823,665

Population growth rate: 0.8%

Urban population: 85.7%

Official language: Portuguese

Religion: Christian

❹ CHILE

Area: 291,933 mi² (756,102 km²)

Capital: Santiago

Population: 17,650,114

Population growth rate: 0.8%

Urban population: 89.5%

Official language: Spanish

Religion: Christian

❺ COLOMBIA

Area: 439,736 mi² (1,138,910 km²)

Capital: Bogotá

Population: 47,220,856

Population growth rate: 1.02%

Urban population: 76.4%

Official language: Spanish

Religion: Christian

❻ ECUADOR

Area: 109,484 mi² (283,561 km²)

Capital: Quito

Population: 16,080,778

Population growth rate: 1.3%

Urban population: 63.7%

Official language: Spanish

Religion: Christian

❼ GUYANA

Area: 83,000 mi² (214,969 km²)
Capital: Georgetown
Population: 735,909
Population growth rate: 0.2%
Urban population: 28.6%
Official language: English
Religions: Christian, Hindu

❽ PARAGUAY

Area: 157,048 mi² (406,752 km²)
Capital: Asunción
Population: 6,862,812
Population growth rate: 1.2%
Urban population: 59.7%
Official languages: Spanish,
   Guarani
Religion: Christian

❾ PERU

Area: 496,225 mi²
   (1,285,216 km²)
Capital: Lima
Population: 30,741,062
Population growth rate: 0.96%
Urban population: 78.6%
Official languages: Spanish,
   Quechua, Aymara
Religion: Christian

❿ SURINAME

Area: 63,251 mi² (163,820 km²)
Capital: Paramaribo
Population: 585,824
Population growth rate: 1.1%
Urban population: 66.0%
Official language: Dutch
Religions: Christian, Hindu

⓫ URUGUAY

Area: 68,037 mi² (176,215 km²)
Capital: Montevideo
Population: 111,219
Population growth rate: 0.3%
Urban population: 95.3%
Official language: Spanish
Religion: Christian

⓬ VENEZUELA

Area: 352,144 mi² (912,050 km²)
Capital: Caracas
Population: 30,912,302
Population growth rate: 1.3%
Urban population: 89.0%
Official language: Spanish
Religion: Christian

About the Author

Stephen F. Cunha is the chair and professor of geography at Humboldt State University in California. He is also the state coordinator for the National Geographic Bee and co-author of *Our Fifty States,* a children's reference book published by National Geographic. He and his family live near Redwood National Park.

Since 1888, the National Geographic Society has funded more than 12,000 research, exploration, and preservation projects around the world. The Society receives funds from National Geographic Partners, LLC, funded in part by your purchase. A portion of the proceeds from this book supports this vital work. To learn more, visit natgeo.com/info.

For more information, visit nationalgeographic.com, call 1-800-647-5463, or write to the following address:

National Geographic Partners
1145 17th Street N.W.
Washington, D.C. 20036-4688 U.S.A.

Visit us online at nationalgeographic.com/books
For librarians and teachers: ngchildrensbooks.org
More for kids from National Geographic: kids.nationalgeographic.com

For information about special
discounts for bulk purchases, please contact
National Geographic Books Special Sales: specialsales@natgeo.com

For rights or permissions inquiries, please contact
National Geographic Books Subsidiary Rights: bookrights@natgeo.com